A GARDENER'S DIRECTORY OF
ORCHIDS

A GARDENER'S DIRECTORY OF
ORCHIDS

Collecting and cultivating beautiful orchids

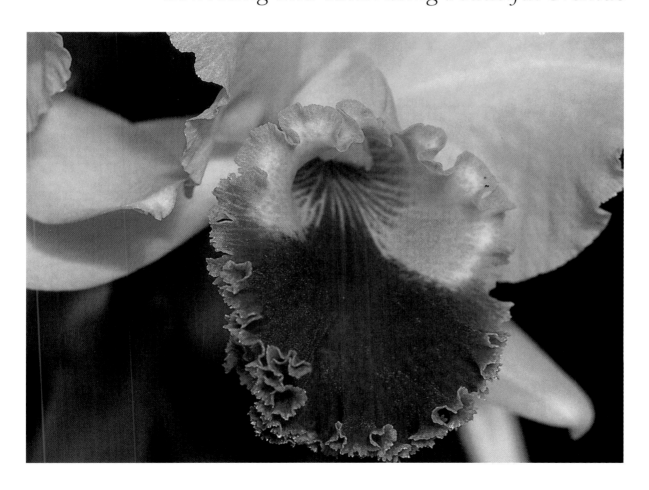

WILMA AND BRIAN RITTERSHAUSEN

SPECIAL PHOTOGRAPHY BY DEREK CRANCH

southwater

This edition is published by Southwater

Distributed in the UK by
The Manning Partnership
251–253 London Road East
Batheaston
Bath BA1 7RL
tel. 01225 852 727
fax 01225 852 852

Published in the USA by
Anness Publishing Inc.
27 West 20th Street
Suite 504
New York
NY 10011
fax 212 807 6813

Distributed in Canada by
General Publishing
895 Don Mills Road
400–402 Park Centre
Toronto, Ontario M3C 1W3
tel. 416 445 3333
fax 416 445 5991

Distributed in Australia by
Sandstone Publishing
Unit 1, 360 Norton Street
Leichhardt
New South Wales 2040
tel. 02 9560 7888
fax 02 9560 7488

Southwater is an imprint of Anness Publishing Limited
Hermes House, 88–89 Blackfriars Road
London SE1 8HA
tel. 020 7401 2077; fax 020 7633 9499

© Anness Publishing Limited 2001

Publisher Joanna Lorenz
Managing Editor Judith Simons
Executive Editor Caroline Davison
Photographers Derek Cranch and Helen Fickling
Designers Ruth Hope and Jane Coney
Jacket Design DW Design
Production Controller Yolande Denny

Previously published as part of a larger compendium,
The Practical Encyclopedia of Orchids

10 9 8 7 6 5 4 3 2 1

Page 1 *Phalaenopsis* Barbara Moler ✕ Spitzberg.
Page 2 *Odontioda* Les Plantons.
Page 3 *Laeliocattleya* Gypsy Queen.
Page 4 *Vuylstekeara* Cambria 'Yellow' (top); *Cymbidium
tracyanum* (centre top); *Coelogyne pandurata* (centre bottom);
Cymbidium Bethlehem 'Ridgeway' (bottom).
Page 5 *Cymbidium* Embers 'Yowie Bay' (top); *Odontioda* Mont
Feland ✕ St Aubin's Bay (centre); *Phalaenopsis* Brother Wild
Thing (bottom).

Contents

THE WORLD OF ORCHIDS

Orchids are grown for the astonishing beauty and variety of their flowers. The most beautiful are the gorgeous South American cattleyas, with their often huge, sparkling, rosy-purple and mauve blooms; these are the aristocrats of the orchid world. Others have an altogether different appeal; these are the strange, sometimes evil-smelling species, which are found among the bulbophyllums in particular. In between these two extremes are numerous delightful orchids of unlimited charm and desirability. It is from among this multitude of varieties that the vast number of collections are made up.

This book sets out to explore the world of orchids from their evolution in the natural world, beginning with an account of how they evolved in the wild, adapting to different situations in fascinating ways. The comprehensive directory which follows includes in-depth background information on each genus, including cultivation requirements. Many of the most popular species are then described in detail, beautiful photographs showing these wonderful plants in their diverse glory.

Cymbidium Lady McAlpine

WHY GROW ORCHIDS?

Orchids can charm and tantalize, fascinate and frustrate. They provide endless satisfaction, as you develop a special bond with a selection of plants that you will need to nurture and care for on a regular basis. Daily spraying, weekly watering and feeding, and constant attention to growing requirements, such as light, warmth and your orchid's general comfort, is a rewarding process. You will soon find that you wish to grow more orchids, and expand your collection to include some rarer orchids, as well as the more popular ones. With time, you will become an expert at growing and caring for your collection, and derive many hours of pleasure just admiring the results of your care and attention.

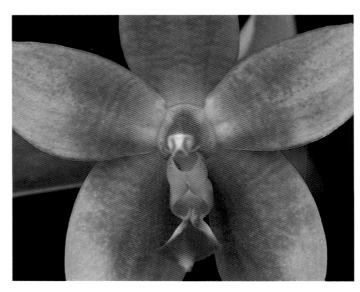

ABOVE *Many delightful hybrids, such as this* Phalaenopsis Sweet Sunrise, *have been bred using the Borneo species* Phalaenopsis violacea *as a starting point. The results are often flowers in extremely rich colours that appear on short flower spikes close to the plant, one bloom at a time.*

FIRST STEPS

Orchids are wonderfully accommodating plants that will succeed in almost any situation with comparative ease. This always astounds those who take their first tentative steps into the world of orchid growing. The reward of seeing the first signs of the developing flower spikes – those small, green shoots at the base of your first orchid – is an exciting event, surpassed only by the eventual opening of the glorious blooms. Often lasting for weeks at a time, these flowers will leave you in no doubt as to the pleasure that orchids can provide.

Orchids are lifelong plants: once acquired they will live for your lifetime and beyond, provided they are not killed accidentally or weakened by mismanagement. Always forgiving, orchids will continue to bloom under the most extreme of conditions, even sacrificing their own lives when a situation becomes intolerable and producing one final burst of colour in a last attempt to perpetuate themselves by seed production.

A century ago, when outrageously high prices were paid for the finest specimens, ensuring that orchids remained the preserve of the wealthy, orchids were considered difficult to grow, requiring specialist skills and the hot, humid atmosphere of a specially structured greenhouse.

Today, orchids are regularly on sale in garden centres, hardware stores and florists, as well as in specialist nurseries, where a wider variety is available. Orchids thrive on windowsills in apartments, offices and hotels, and in the small greenhouses of the serious hobby-growers.

Three Popular Orchids

The one orchid you will meet most often in homegrown situations is the delightful *Phalaenopsis*, softly hued, speckled or spotted, candy-striped or plain. In recent years these orchids have shot to fame and are now the most popular houseplant orchid. In white, pink and yellow colour combinations, phalaenopsis produce three to four attractive, dark to mid-green, broad, horizontally curving leaves, with thick, silvery white roots that have a strong tendency to meander outside their pot.

LEFT *The superb flowers of* Miltoniopsis *Faldouet have red-maroon petals and white lips, which are edged with mauve and streaked and spotted with maroon.*

Many other orchids will also thrive indoors with the minimum of care, but few can compare with the beautiful miltoniopsis, or pansy orchids as they are affectionately known. Their small plant size and large, decorative blooms create a summer show with a delicate fragrance. Look out for these orchids and similar adaptable kinds in your local outlet, and take one or two home. You will not be disappointed.

While it will not take you long to get to know and recognize these popular orchids, it will take a lifetime to learn about them generally, for there are far more of them than any other plant, and it is this endless search for further knowledge to understand the largest plant family in the world that makes orchid growing so totally absorbing.

Usually bought in flower, these will last for weeks at a time, and, before the first flower spike has finished, there is often another showing at the base with the promise of further blooms in the months to come. These plants are ideally suited to indoor culture, where they are unlikely to be exposed to the direct sun, caught in a cold draught or left to freeze on cold nights. The home is a place of warmth and comfort, which suits these tropical epiphytic orchids perfectly.

One further orchid that is frequently seen gracing large open areas is the *Cymbidium*. At home indoors or in the greenhouse, these robust orchids produce long, narrow, tropical-looking foliage that typically cascades below the blooms, which are carried on tall flower spikes with a dozen or more flowers. With almost unlimited colours available, there is no end to their variety: only blue has proved elusive

to the hybridizer. Cymbidiums mostly bloom in winter and spring, bursting into flower at a time when their vibrant shades and pastel colourings are a welcome contrast to the bare gardens outside. Their blooms will remain in perfect condition for months on end.

RIGHT *The lateral petals of* Cymbidium erythrostylum, *a delightful species from Vietnam, are thrust forward to hug the lip. The perfect, pristine-white blooms have produced some excellent hybrids.*

ORCHIDS IN THE WILD

Orchids represent the largest family of flowering plants in the world, and their diversity and distribution are virtually unchallenged in the plant kingdom. Every land habitat where it is possible for a plant to grow will contain orchids. They thrive on windswept mountain tops and in steaming tropical jungles. They cling to niches in the bitterly cold Arctic regions and in the hottest, driest deserts.

THE EVOLUTION OF ORCHIDS

A wide range of environments, from the seashore to the high alpine line, provide habitats for indigenous orchids. Within this global distribution, we find some 25,000 to 30,000 species. Since the beginning of modern plant classification, started by the Swedish naturalist Linnaeus in 1758, to the present day, taxonomists have continued to classify and reclassify existing species, as well as describing new ones. Every year, from some corner of the world, come new discoveries of orchid species. Some are so startlingly beautiful that it is hard to understand how they have remained undetected for so long, while others are so inconspicuous that it is clear why they have been overlooked. China, for example, is a huge country only recently opened up to Western exploration, and this has resulted in the discovery of some incredible *Paphiopedilum* species.

In addition to the vast number of species, there are some 100,000 man-made hybrids – a number that increases annually, as hybridizers the world over endeavour to meet an insatiable demand for more varieties. So great is

the variation, it seems unbelievable that they can all belong to the same family of plants, which are classified according to the structure of their flowers and their resemblance to one another.

Orchid Distribution

It is their extremely small, dust-like seed that has enabled orchids to disperse and travel such great distances. Carried on the wind across continents and oceans,

ABOVE *New species of orchids are continually being discovered. In the latter part of the 20th century, some amazing, new paphiopedilums came to light in China, such as the golden yellow* Paphiopedilum armeniacum. *Nothing like it had been seen in the genus before.*

the seeds have helped orchids to colonize the world. Cypripediums, for example, are found circling the top of the globe in a line just below the Arctic Circle. Their far-reaching habitat has contributed to the emergence of many different species. Due to their often harsh habitats, some are extremely slow-growing, but once established in large populations they can exist for many years until they are disturbed.

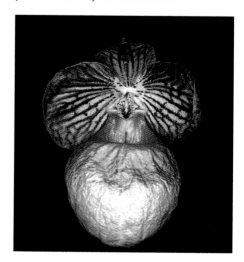

ABOVE *The beautifully striped and coloured species* Paphiopedilum micranthum *carries a huge, bulbous pouch which is quite untypical of the genus. Another recent discovery from China, it has produced a whole new range of hybrids.*

ABOVE *Orchid seeds are minute, no larger than very fine sawdust. Magnified hundreds of times, the fertile embryo of these* Liparis unata *seeds can be seen inside a protective covering. Seed capsules can contain anything up to half a million seeds.*

Ten thousand years ago, the last Ice Age covered much of the globe in a freezing grip. This huge shield of frozen water stretched from the North Pole, covering much of the Northern Hemisphere. This must have forced the orchids back from their original occupation of the land. Within the last few thousand years, as the ice shield receded, the orchids advanced again to regain the territories that they had occupied before the big freeze. In this way, the northern orchids have been moved backwards and forwards as a result of these dramatic climate changes. This has had a direct impact on their evolution. However, the tropical orchids in the forests close to the Equator remained largely unaffected by such climatic changes. The rainforests have hardly changed for millions of years. This has allowed the orchids to evolve without interruption, resulting in the greatest diversity to be found in these regions.

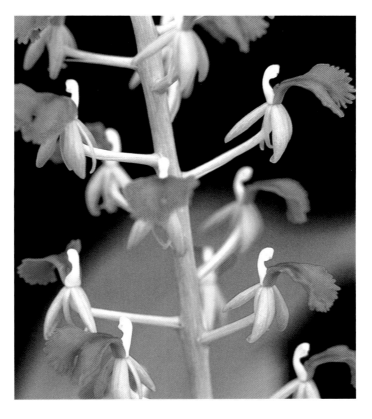

LEFT *Although the tiny, brightly coloured blooms of* Liparis unata *are just 1cm (¹/₂in) across, they are produced on flower spikes, which are 30cm (12in) tall. The sight of a large plant with several flower spikes is a sheer delight.*

LEFT Coelogyne mooreana 'Brockhurst' FCC/RHS *is a superb species from Vietnam. It is unrivalled for its pristine white flowers which are enhanced by the deep golden lip. These plants grow well in cultivation and are all descended from a single clone which was imported into Britain around the turn of the 20th century.*

ABOVE *There are numerous orchids that are small enough to fit into a thimble.* Schoenorchis pachyrachis, *a species from Malaysia, produces its tiny flowers in profusion. Its small stature makes it ideal for growing on bark.*

Orchids and Other Organisms

In order to survive climate changes, orchids have evolved strange associations with other living organisms. Co-existing within the root structure of most orchids is a microscopic fungus (mycelium). This alliance forms a symbiotic relationship, whereby both the orchid and the fungus become completely dependent upon each other for their survival. The mycelium releases nutrients that are absorbed by the orchid, which in turn becomes the host for the fungus. Most orchids have their own specific micro-fungi, so there must exist as many different fungi as there are orchids. For a seed to germinate, it needs contact with the fungus from the beginning. For this reason, orchids are often found in large colonies, rather than growing as individual plants, because this close proximity to other orchids ensures that the necessary fungus is present.

Tropical epiphytes will also only grow on particular species of trees. In dense rainforest that has remained undisturbed for centuries, it is only certain trees that play host. The larger, more bulky orchids are confined to the main trunk or the first fork of a very large tree, while the smaller species will cling to the finer twigs and branches higher up on the outskirts of the canopy. As the leaf cover increases and becomes denser in evergreen forests, the orchids at the centre of such cover produce healthier and darker-foliaged specimens, but may not be as free-flowering as those growing on the edge. Here the plants will benefit from cooling prevailing winds and extra sunlight, flowering better as a result, although often with shrivelling pseudobulbs and yellowing foliage.

BELOW LEFT *A bluebottle is attracted to this* Bulbophyllum *species by the lurid red lip, which resembles an open animal wound. As it pushes deeper into the "wound", the hinged lip will catapult the fly's body against the pollinia.*

BELOW *This fly is attracted to a* Gongora *species by its appearance. Note the highly specialized pollinating mechanism which ensures the fly will be guided to the pollinia.*

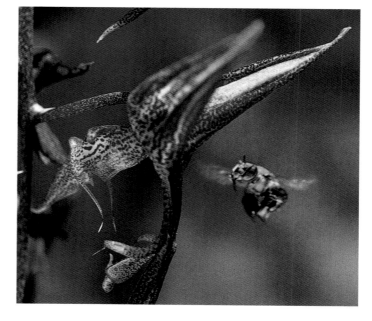

RIGHT *This* Hexisea bidentata *from South America is being pollinated by a humming bird. This accounts for the flower being all red with no other decoration. Instead, it entices the bird with nectar.*

To achieve pollination, orchid flowers have also developed special relationships with insects, humming-birds and even small bats. In the case of insects, the relationship is formed with a group of insects or just one specific species. The insect is attracted to the bloom in its search for nectar, which is sometimes, but not always, given in return for facilitating pollination. The colour, shape and size of the flower are all significant forms of attraction. Many use mimicry to attract a certain bee or fly, and this is seen in the European species of *Ophrys*, where the lip of the flower resembles the female of the species; the male, believing it has found a mate, attempts copulation, but succeeds instead in pollinating the flower. In the bee orchid (*Ophrys apifera*), the orchid times the opening of its flowers to coincide with the emergence of the male bees, which appear on the wing about three weeks before the females. Once the females emerge, the male bee will lose interest in the flowers. The timing of this flowering is therefore critical for pollination.

There are some orchids, particularly among the *Bulbophyllum* species, that emit a strong odour of putrefaction. These have sepals or a lip in a dark reddish colour that resembles decaying meat, just the place where carrion flies and wasps would normally lay their eggs. In contrast, other orchids such as *Brassavola nodosa* carry a delicious night-time scent, relying on night-flying moths and other nocturnal insects for pollination. There are also the fabulous angraecums, which produce mainly white flowers that release their perfume only in the early part of the day to coincide with the time when their specific insect is active. Other species, such as *Oncidium flexuosum*, produce their flowers in a closely-clustered swarm at the end of a long, thin flower spike, which will attract little flying insects by the movement of the slightest breeze.

The unique partnership between orchids and their specific pollinators has evolved over an extremely long period of time, but it can be easily broken by man's unwarranted interference with the natural world through the indiscriminate misuse of insecticides, the felling of trees and the spread of agriculture.

LEFT *Burnet moths are attracted to the flowers of the terrestrial* Anacamptis pyramidalis. *The flowers are slightly fragrant, but carry no nectar.*

TYPES OF ORCHID

There are a number of different types of orchid which are classified according to the way they live and survive, whether they are supported by trees or rocks or grow in the ground. Some orchids have adapted to survive in different conditions.

Epiphytes

Those orchids that have evolved to live upon trees are called epiphytes. These are not the same as parasites, which owe their existence to nourishment taken out of the tree. Epiphytes take nothing from the tree upon which they grow, but merely take advantage of a loftier lifestyle and gain benefit from being closer to the air and light than the vegetation growing on the forest floor. This aerial way of life is not restricted to orchids, and they share this existence with bromeliads, ferns and mosses and other plants that creep along the branches, creating their own micro-climate high in the tree canopy. One further advantage of living in the tree canopy is the abundance of insect life, which is needed to pollinate the flowers. Orchids have found many ways of attracting specific pollinators to their flowers.

Epiphytes obtain their nutrients from the moisture in the air, and from any debris that has collected in the axils of the branches or beneath mosses where their roots will penetrate. Decomposing leaf litter and bird or animal droppings will make up the remainder of their meagre diet. Various epiphytic orchids have utilized every part of preferred trees. Some cling to the larger branches close to the main trunk, or hug the trunk itself, often growing to huge proportions that completely encircle the tree. Sometimes, the sheer weight of a two-ton mammoth orchid (*Grammatophyllum speciosum*) can make the tree crash to the ground. Other orchids, called twig epiphytes, cling precariously to the extremities of the branches, while some, such as *Psygmorchis pusilla*, even germinate and grow on the leaves of certain trees in Central America.

Being dependent upon the host tree, the orchids adapt a similar lifestyle. When the trees shed their leaves at the onset of the dry season to conserve moisture, many of the orchids do the same. Their aerial roots cease to grow and the growing tips become covered by the white velamen that protects them from damage and dehydration. Their growing season finished, the orchids remain in a dormant state until the onset of the first rains, which herald a new start when the plants become active once again. While the

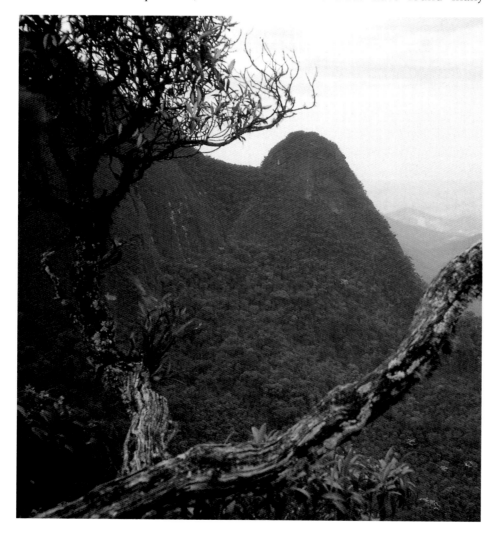

LEFT *High up on the ridges that overlook these deep, lush valleys, epiphytic orchids cling to the exposed twigs. The weather conditions can be quite inhospitable, and the orchids must contend with the strong winds, rain and low temperatures of the Brazilian rainy season.*

ABOVE The scarlet flowers of the epiphytic Sophronitis coccinea *sparkle like bright gems on the trees of the high ridges of the Brazilian coastal forest where they can be shrouded in clouds for days at a time.*

orchids are resting, they rely upon the stored moisture in their pseudobulbs to maintain them. After prolonged periods of drought, these pseudobulbs will begin to shrivel; this is a normal yearly process for many orchids.

With the start of the rainy season, new growth commences and new roots soon follow. The roots take up moisture to fill out the pseudobulbs once again. The newly developing growths rely upon the older, mature pseudobulbs for their source of energy until their own roots can nourish them. The ageing pseudobulbs will support the newer growths until they become exhausted and, in a dried and shrivelled state, eventually die. By this time, numerous new pseudobulbs will have taken their place, and in this way orchids can, in theory, live forever. In practice, they will thrive for hundreds of years, or for as long as their host tree remains standing.

For reasons not fully understood, many epiphytes select a specific tree on which to grow. This may be due to the texture of the bark in which they root, or it may reflect the nutrients available in the old bark. Likewise, some orchid species will only grow on one side of a tree, perhaps away from the prevailing wind.

ABOVE LEFT The tops of mountains in high-altitude areas, such as in the coastal Brazilian forest, can be covered in clouds for many days. This makes the area constantly moist from the dew that forms within the clouds.

BELOW The epiphytic species Scuticaria hadwenii *is a lovely orchid to see high up in a tree, with its long, terete leaves hanging down. It is fairly well camouflaged among the other forest plants.*

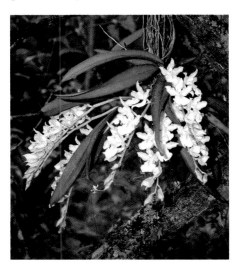

LEFT The beautiful epiphytic species Rodriguezia bractiata *from Brazil grows abundantly on fruit trees where the cascading white flowers look like snow in early spring.*

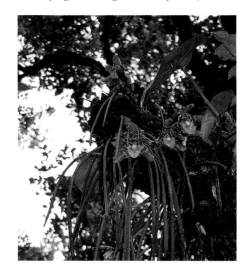

While epiphytes dwell upon living trees, a few orchids, such as the *Catasetum* species, are saprophytic, living upon decaying trees, where their roots penetrate the softer tissue beneath the bark. Their lifespan is more limited than that of the epiphytes, because dead trees in the tropics will remain for only a few years before fungi and termites take their toll. Therefore the saprophytes must be fast-growing and produce seed quickly so that the next generation can move on to other habitats.

Terrestrials

These orchids grow in the ground, and there is hardly any area where terrestrial orchids have not adapted to grow. They are found in places as diverse as the hot, dry Australian deserts, to the

shadier and gentler climates of temperate woodlands and grasslands. In North America, orchids such as the delightful *Cypripedium calceolus* grow in the cool forests, and other *Cypripedium* species are found in areas of Russia extending to the very edge of the Arctic Circle.

LEFT *The fragrant* Zygopetalum crinitum *enjoys a shady position away from the bright Brazilian sunshine. Many of these plants are found growing terrestrially under the trees.*

Terrestrial orchids may be found in solitary splendour or with just a few in a colony, while in other locations they appear in their thousands, tinting a grassy meadow purple or pink with their flower spikes (species of *Orchis* and *Dactylorhiza*). Among the terrestrial orchids there is as much variation as can be found among the tropical epiphytes. However, they have not excited the collector in the same way as the epiphytes, mainly because they are less easy to cultivate and less flamboyant in their plants as well as their flowers.

Typically, the terrestrial orchids grow a single leafy stem which rises from one or two underground tubers, or a mass of rhizomatous roots. These can grow either just below the surface of the natural grass-covering or deep in the soil, depending upon the conditions. The stem terminates in the flowering head, which may have from one to many blooms. While some species grow in sandy soils in arid places, others flourish in marshy swamps, where their tubers remain submerged in water for much of the year. During the winter, only the underground parts of the plant survive to reactivate new growth in the spring. Other terrestrials, such as *Phaius* and the evergreen calanthes, produce a creeping rhizome with pseudobulbs

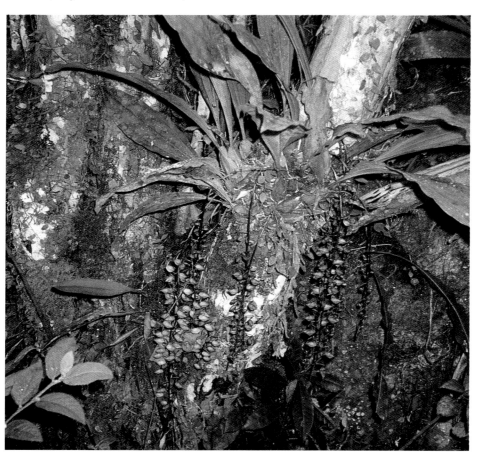

LEFT *Growing near the base of a large tree, this* Gongora bufonia *will be a fantastic sight when its 11 flower spikes open and attract swarms of euglossan bees to pollinate it.*

RIGHT *This is a typical scene on a bromeliad-covered ridge in the Atlantic Forest of Brazil. Bromeliads are huge plants which grow on both the trees and the ground. Their centres are filled with water, which is a vital source of humidity. A* Scuticaria hadwenii *flowers in the centre.*

at ground level. The root system penetrates deep into the soil to find moisture and nutrients.

Not all terrestrial orchids with underground rhizomes live in cold areas. Many of the tropical species adopt this way of life, becoming completely deciduous and remaining dormant below ground level during the dry season. Their green parts emerge when conditions are suitable. These different habitats often merge, and epiphytes that fall from their host trees will, where conditions are suitable, be perfectly at home on the ground. Equally, terrestrial orchid seeds that have settled on mossy branches can find a suitable roothold and become established there. These orchids are great opportunists, and will grow well wherever conditions suit them. Stanhopeas and acinetas are epiphytes that produce pendent flower spikes. If they should end up on the ground, the plants will grow but are unable to bloom, because their flower spikes penetrate the soil and perish.

A few terrestrial orchids, such as *Bletia* species, produce pseudobulbs, and many of the species within the genus *Pleione* are also considered

RIGHT *Wet, boggy areas have formed on this rock which has a constant flow of water running across it. Held secure by tough grasses, and in bud, are large clumps of* Epidendrum aquaticum, *which loves having its roots in the water.*

terrestrial, although they too produce pseudobulbs; these remain above the surface of the ground, or become covered by the mosses and lichens among which they grow.

While the terrestrial species of Europe share many characteristics, in Australia some of the strangest types have evolved that have no comparison anywhere. The Australian terrestrials are worthy of study in their own right, but these plants are not generally found in cultivation, and knowledge of them outside Australia is gleaned mostly from other specialist publications.

Although the terrestrial orchids are not cultivated, they still have enthusiasts who would seek them out, returning each year to a favourable location to search for them in bogs, on hillsides and wherever else they may appear. These devotees are armed not with spades to dig them up but with cameras to photograph each individual and build up their own records

RIGHT *These seedlings of* Oncidium blanchetii *have been reintroduced into the wild in their native South-east Brazil to try to increase their diminishing numbers. These seedlings have all thrived and are now showing their flower spikes.*

of flowering data. For many orchid enthusiasts, the opportunity of searching and observing tropical orchids in the wild is an unattainable goal, but where there is the easier option of finding terrestrial orchids, the satisfaction generated is just as great.

One aspect that makes this so compelling year after year is the fluctuation in the number of flowering plants that may arise. In an area supporting hundreds of flowering plants in one season, you may be hard pressed to find a dozen the next. Terrestrial orchids are notorious for appearing sporadically over the seasons, and some species of *Orchis* can remain in a dormant state underground for many years before suddenly reappearing. In neglected gardens, unmown lawns can support many orchids where previously the lawnmower had decapitated the flowers. When prevented from flowering, orchids increase their vegetative growth below grass level, becoming more vigorous, so when the opportunity arises, they create an even better show of blooms. Where such plants are found in a lawn, do not treat the grass with selective weedkillers, or you will lose them.

Many of the terrestrial orchids use deception to attract insects to pollinate their flowers. In the genus *Ophrys*, commonly known as bee or spider orchids, the lip of the flower of certain species resembles either a bee or a spider closely enough to fool the male of the species into believing it is a female. While the bee or spider mounts the flower and endeavours to copulate, it receives or deposits pollen which is then delivered from one flower to another.

Terrestrial orchids are found worldwide, but many, like the epiphytes, are becoming increasingly rare in the wild, where habitats are being destroyed through urbanization, the spread of agriculture, mining or quarrying, or the application of fertilizer to improve grassland.

ABOVE *Some orchids, such as the terrestrial* Paphiopedilum gratrixianum *from Laos, have evolved specialized "pouches" in order to trap pollinating insects.*

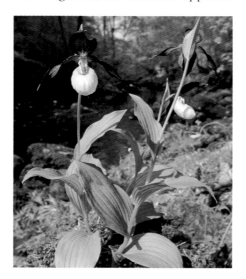

ABOVE Cypripedium calceolus, *a lady's slipper orchid, is a hardy terrestrial which originates from Europe and North America.*

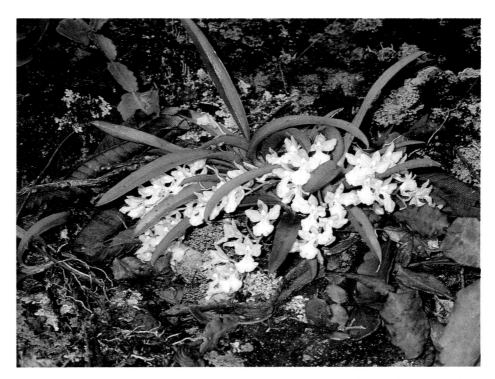

Lithophytes

Performing a balancing act somewhere between the epiphytes inhabiting the trees and the terrestrials in the soil are the lithophytes. These orchids make their homes on rocky cliff faces, sometimes on near vertical slopes where conditions are too extreme for much other plant life. Often these are limestone cliffs near to the seashore, or moss-covered rocks where there is some protection for the roots. The plants will find any small crevice where they can gain a hold, and cling on with their strong roots. The inaccessibility of some lithophytic habitats has allowed a few noteworthy orchids, such as *Phragmipedium besseae*, to remain undiscovered until recently, being detected only from the air.

Lithophytes obtain their nourishment in a similar way to epiphytes, relying upon regular mists and rain for moisture, but also having to withstand long periods of extreme dryness. Extra moisture and nutrients are obtained

ABOVE LEFT *The species* Cytopodium andersoniae *is managing to thrive by growing on this smooth, flat rock surface. It makes a striking sight with its long, tapering leaves.*

from roots that meander and penetrate into the crevices in the rocks, or underneath the mossy covering. Orchids that grow in this way include the pleiones and some species of *Paphiopedilum*. Often species that are epiphytic close to, or around, the base of trees become lithophytic when a suitable opportunity arises. Likewise, the terrestrial species of *Paphiopedilum* will also graduate onto surrounding rocks, where there is a sufficient covering of mosses or humus for their roots to remain covered.

In cultivation, lithophytes are treated in the same way as epiphytes. There are many examples among the hybrids, particularly with paphiopedilums and phragmipediums, of epiphytic species being crossed with lithophytic or terrestrial species within the same genus.

ABOVE Rodriguezia bractiata *is seen here unusually growing on a large boulder where it has landed after falling from the tree above. It has continued to grow successfully, surrounded by lichens.*

ABOVE Stenoglottis fimbriata *is a terrestrial orchid from South Africa.*

ORCHID DIRECTORY

We have seen that the orchid family is extremely diverse and so vast that no single work can cover them all. The following section describes and illustrates those orchids that make up the most popular types grown today. Here you will find

recommendations for the beginner, challenges for the serious grower, and other orchids that may be hard to find in cultivation but that have been given a special mention to illustrate the huge differences between the flowers of this amazingly variable family. Every plant, with the exception of the native British orchids, has been grown by the authors, and the descriptions and notes are drawn from personal experience of knowing and growing these undeniably lovely plants.

Explore the world of orchids further and you will encounter many more than are listed here. In time, you will develop your own favourite varieties, and as your knowledge progresses so your orchid collection will become more specialized, housing those that appeal directly to you and that you find easiest to grow. The following selection is just a starting point from which to set out on your voyage of discovering new orchids for yourself.

Phalaenopsis Little Skipper 'Zuma Nova'

POPULAR ORCHIDS

The orchids listed here are suitable for a range of temperatures and situations. The pot sizes given are for adult plants, while the height is for adult plants that are not in flower.

BRASSIA

This small naturally occurring genus of evergreen epiphytic plants originates from Central and South America, including the West Indies. A few of the 25 species are in cultivation and there are a limited number of hybrids. Some startling results have been obtained by intergeneric breeding with odontoglossums and others in this alliance. The results are often large, dramatic flowers with soft colourings, as can be seen in the hybrid genus *Maclellanara*, which combines *Brassia* with *Odontoglossum* and *Oncidium*.

The species are characterized by the extremely long and narrow petals and sepals, which give rise to the common name of spider orchids. The main colourings are light green and brown. The plants have oval, green pseudobulbs and usually two, though occasionally one, mid-green leaves. The flower spikes appear from the base of the leading pseudobulb in spring and carry up to a dozen flowers on two distinct planes, on arching spikes well above the foliage. The flowering time is early summer, and the flowers, which are wonderfully scented, will last for four to five weeks.

Brassias do well in the company of odontoglossums or in a mixed collection. The plants can be divided when they are

Brassia verrucosa

large enough, and propagation is from back bulbs.

Temperature: Mainly cool-growing.
Cultivation: Grow in 10–15cm (4–6in) pots of bark-based compost (growing medium) or on bark. Water all year, but more moderately in winter. Spray foliage in summer, but keep the buds and flowers dry.
Height: To 30cm (12in).

Brassia Edvah Loo 'Vera Cruz' AM/RHS
The amazingly long – 15cm (6in) or more – sepals and petals on this very fine, awarded hybrid have been produced by crossing the orange-tinted *Brassia longissima* with a further long-petalled species, *B. gireoudiana*. This plant will do best in a warm greenhouse.

Brassia Rex
This older hybrid originated in Hawaii from the green-flowered *Brassia verrucosa* and *B. gireoudiana*. The plant is heat tolerant, making it suitable for cultivation in the warmer parts of the United States and elsewhere.

Brassia verrucosa
The wonderfully long, 15cm (6in) symmetrical flowers of this easily grown species from Honduras and elsewhere ensure its continued popularity as a cool-growing plant for the home or greenhouse. The fragrant flowers appear in early summer.

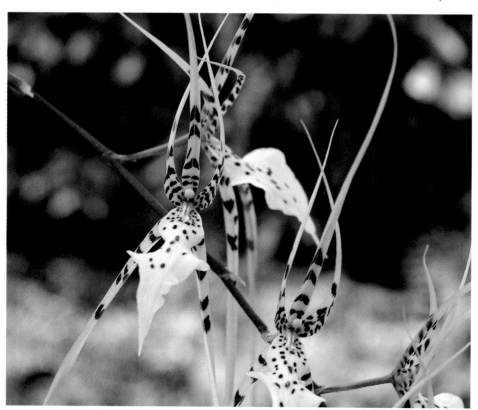

Brassia Edvah Loo 'Vera Cruz' AM/RHS

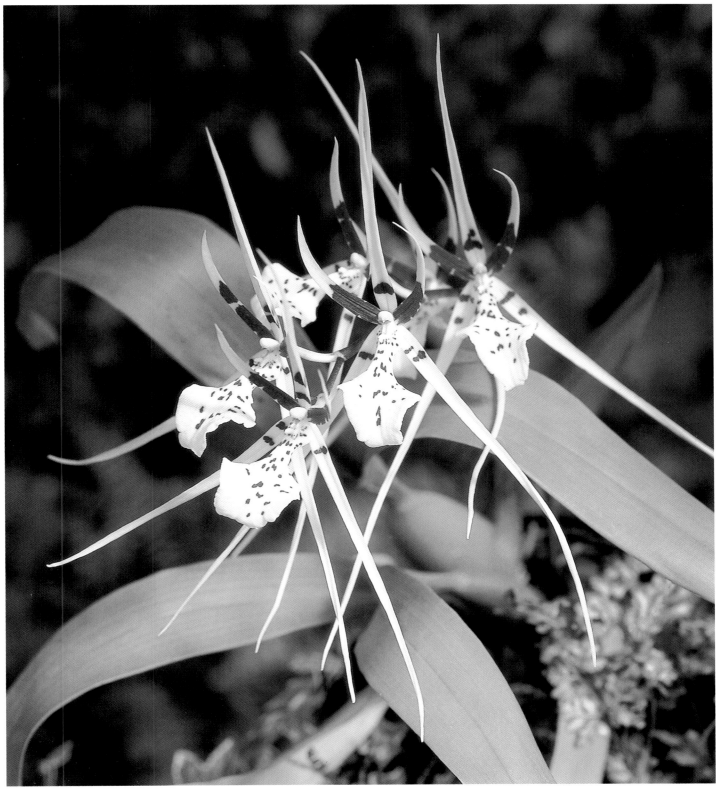

Brassia Rex

CATTLEYA ALLIANCE

Cattleyas were the earliest of the showy, tropical epiphytic orchids to be grown and flowered in cultivation. The first was *Cattleya labiata*, introduced from the mountainous forests of Brazil in 1818. Cattleyas form part of a huge alliance comprising many other related orchids, the best known of the natural genera being *Laelia, Brassavola, Sophronitis* and *Encyclia*. These, and others, have been widely interbred for nearly 200 years to produce the colossal range of variously sized flowers that is available. The species in the alliance originate from Central and South America, and in the genus *Cattleya* there are about 50 species. Most of these are rare in the wild and are found in cultivation in specialist collections, where they have been raised in nurseries from selected clones.

Hybrids can be counted in their thousands, and range from miniature plants containing species of the diminutive *Sophronitis*, mostly with brightly coloured flowers in orange, yellow and red, to the large, frilled excesses of the *Brassavola* crosses. The most well known of these man-made hybrids are *Sophrolaeliocattleya, Brassolaeliocattleya* and *Laeliocattleya*. These names can easily be unravelled to identify the specific genera as *Sophronitis, Brassavola, Laelia* and *Cattleya*, but when more than three genera are involved, the name given to the resulting cross is personalized to one individual, making the name less clear on the label. *Potinara*, for example, is the result of crossing *Brassavola, Cattleya, Laelia* and *Sophronitis*.

With such a complex alliance, it becomes impossible to describe the typical "cattleya", although all related hybrids are loosely referred to collectively as cattleyas, whatever their make-up.

Among the *Cattleya* species are two distinct groups. These are the unifoliate, which have one leaf, and the bifoliate, which have two. All are evergreen, shedding just an occasional back leaf from time to time. These two groups are well defined in their flowers. The unifoliate species are known for the glistening beauty of their large, frilly-lipped blooms whose dominant colours are white through pink and yellow to exquisite rose-lavender and mauve shades. The bifoliate species have mostly smaller flowers, some with waxy petals and sepals and less frilly lips. Here, other colours, such as green and brown, are found, and the flowers are often heavily spotted or speckled.

Cattleyas produce mostly elongated or club-shaped pseudobulbs, often sheathed while young, with stiffened, dark green leaves. The flower buds are produced from the apex of the pseudobulb, usually encased in a protective sheath, which dries and splits to allow the developing buds to emerge. While most produce their blooms on short spikes, hybrids containing the Mexican species of *Laelia*, such as *L. anceps*, have longer flower spikes.

In most of the fragrant orchid species, the scent becomes lost with hybridizing, but among the *Cattleya* alliance, this fragrance is retained in the vast majority of hybrids, which adds to their allure.

Cattleyas are very much flowers of fashion. During the early and middle part of the last century, the goal was to breed ever larger flowers, which were worn by society ladies. For the grower, the huge heads of blooms required staking to prevent the stems from bending under their own weight. With the popularizing of the smaller flowers achieved by breeding with *Sophronitis*, and the bright colours that appeared, these more easily accommodated hybrids became an instant success with growers. Today, there is still an enormous range of flower types, with something to suit all tastes in this fabulous alliance.

Cattleyas like good light. However, the stiffened foliage is deceptive, and the early spring sunshine can quickly burn their leaves if they are not protected from direct sun. Most cattleyas have a dormant resting period, but this varies from plant to plant. It is not unusual for some to start their new growth in the autumn and continue to grow throughout the winter. The rule is to watch your plant, and when it is not actively in growth, allow it to remain on the dry side until new growth is seen.

Cattleyas make copious roots, which are a joy when they explode from the base of the newly formed pseudobulb. The thick, creeping, woody rhizome connecting the pseudobulbs often results in the development of new growths over the rim of the pot, and, when the new roots follow, this can be a problem for the grower. Although the roots will grow well outside the pot, they can become a problem when the plant is repotted, and will need to be cut back to avoid them becoming rotten. The timing is crucial: repot as soon as the new growth has developed to a stage where the new roots can just be seen, but have not grown sufficiently to be damaged. At this stage, the older roots can be trimmed back with less shock to the plant.

Brassolaeliocattleya Dorothy Bertsch 'Buttercup'

Brassolaeliocattleya Malworth × *Laeliocattleya* Honigmond

Temperature: Intermediate-growing.
Cultivation: Grow in pots of 15–20cm
(6–8in) or less in coarse bark compost
(growing medium) or Rockwool. Water well
in summer, and give little water in winter.
Mist foliage in summer. Keep shaded in
summer, and give full light in winter.
Height: 15cm (6in) or less to 45cm (18in)
and above.

Brassolaeliocattleya Mem. Dorothy Bertsch 'Buttercup'

This *Cattleya*-type hybrid has a perfect
shape and form. The glistening, apricot-
coloured flowers are 15cm (6in) across.
Usually one, but occasionally two, flowers
are produced in summer.

Brassolaeliocattleya Malworth × *Laeliocattleya* Honigmond

This fragrant, autumn-flowering hybrid is
a combination of *Brassavola*, *Laelia* and
Cattleya. All three genera have contributed
something of value to this hybrid. The
pink flowers are enhanced by the yellow
throat at the centre of the lip.

Cattleya Andean Mist

This pure white *Cattleya* has been line-
bred through successive generations of
white-flowered species, such as *Cattleya
mossiae* var. *alba*, to maintain the clearest
colour form. One to three 10cm (4in)
fragrant flowers are produced during
the summer.

Cattleya Andean Mist

Cattleya skinneri

Laeliocattleya Archange

Cattleya Golden Girl
The bright orange colouring of this autumn-flowering hybrid grex has only been achieved by generations of selective breeding. This has produced a good-size bloom with a strong colour.

Cattleya skinneri
Heralded as the national flower of Costa Rica, this delightful, autumn-flowering species was first collected in Guatemala in 1838. It was discovered by the orchid hunter George Ure-Skinner, after whom it was named. Several colour forms are seen, including white. The plant has been extensively hybridized.

Laeliocattleya Archange
This large-flowered, frilly, pink hybrid shows exquisite depth of colour in the lip. These flowers appear in spring from the previous season's mature pseudobulbs.

Laeliocattleya Beaumesnil 'Parme'
The *Cattleya* parent has influenced the shape of this charming hybrid, which produces a head of two to four large, scented, yellow-centred, mauve flowers during the summer months. The flowers are compact with neat, semi-enclosed lips.

Cattleya Golden Girl

Laeliocattleya Beaumesnil 'Parme'

Laeliocattleya Carrie Johnson

This cream and crimson hybrid has peloric markings on the petals that repeat the lip markings. The flower shape resembles the *Laelia anceps* parent, with the blooms on a long stem. The *Laelia* influence allows the plant to be grown cool, indoors or in a greenhouse, where it blooms in late spring.

Laeliocattleya Chit Chat 'Tangerine'

Flocks of 5cm (2in) bright orange flowers adorn this pretty, spring-flowering hybrid, which has been raised from the brightly coloured species *Cattleya aurantiaca* from Guatemala and the equally vibrant Brazilian species *Laelia cinnabarina* and *L. harpophylla*. The latter two were crossed in 1902 to give *Laelia* Coronet.

Laeliocattleya Gypsy Queen

This American hybrid displays all the qualities looked for in the largest-flowered *Cattleya* alliance blooms. Gorgeously frilled, these huge, pale pink, 10cm (4in) blooms have red lips and yellow centres. They will last for a good three weeks during the summer.

Laeliocattleya Magic Bell 'New Trick'

These charming little flowers, 7cm (3in) across, are produced in autumn on a neat, compact plant with slender pseudobulbs and two leaves. With *Cattleya aurantiaca* in its background, giving the open shape and colouring, this hybrid is unusual for its bi-coloured petals and sepals.

Laeliocattleya Carrie Johnson

Laeliocattleya Magic Bell 'New Trick'

Laeliocattleya Chit Chat 'Tangerine'

Laeliocattleya Gypsy Queen

Sophrolaeliocattleya Jewel Box 'Dark Waters'

Laeliocattleya Pomme d'Or

This hybrid carries smaller flowers with a fleshier texture, which are more abundant on the spike. The rich yellow colouring and red veining in the throat of the lip is a winning combination. This is a spring- and autumn-blooming plant, which lasts for a good three weeks.

Laeliocattleya Starting Point 'Unique'

The exquisite, semi-alba varieties, such as this superb, large-flowered, autumn-flowering hybrid, are hard to resist. The sharply contrasting deep purple lip is framed by the pristine white of the sepals and petals. This is a robust grower that originates from California.

Sophrolaeliocattleya Jewel Box 'Dark Waters'

Clusters of crimson, 7cm (3in) flowers adorn this variety of Jewel Box, which has been inspired by the vivid colour of the *Sophronitis*, while the shape is reminiscent of the *Laelia*. This neat grower easily becomes a specimen plant by continually "breaking double", that is, producing several new growths from one pseudobulb. The flowers appear in spring.

Laeliocattleya Pomme d'Or

Laeliocattleya Starting Point 'Unique'

COELOGYNE

This is a natural genus of evergreen, epiphytic plants found over a wide area in India, China and throughout most of Malaysia. Those that are found in the Himalayas require cool house treatment and make ideal houseplants. The Malaysian types, which are often larger in growth, are suitable for a slightly higher temperature range. There is a good number of species in cultivation as well as a handful of hybrids, some made many years ago and still highly regarded.

The main colouring in this genus is pristine white with a highly decorated lip; the flowers are often accompanied by a sweet fragrance. Light tawny brown and green are also represented in the colour range. The variably sized plants produce green pseudobulbs, plump and shiny when young, wrinkled when old, which may be less than 2.5cm (1in) high, or over 15cm (6in) tall. Between these two extremes are some truly delightful plants, ideal for windowsill culture or small greenhouses. All support a pair of narrow, oval leaves and most produce their flower spikes from the young growth. The flower spikes can be extremely short and single-flowered, or long and drooping, with a chain of up to two dozen blooms. Coelogynes bloom during late winter and spring, and all are well worth growing.

Coelogynes have well-defined growing and resting periods. Some shrivelling of the pseudobulbs usually occurs during dormancy, which is normal, but they should plump up again when the plant resumes its growth. A number of the species are ideal for growing on into specimen plants – including *Coelogyne cristata*, which can grow to huge proportions – and massive plants are often seen at shows throughout the spring, supporting a frothing mass of effervescent, stunning white flowers.

Coelogyne corymbosa

Temperature: Cool- to intermediate-growing.
Cultivation: Grow in 7–15cm (3–6in) pots depending on the species. Water and feed regularly from spring onwards as the new growth appears. Reduce watering as winter approaches. Keep well-shaded in summer and give full light in winter.
Height: 15–45cm (6–18in).

Coelogyne asperata

This large-growing species from Malaya can reach a height of 60cm (2ft), although the flowers appear on shorter, arching flower spikes. The straw-yellow flowers, which reach 7cm (3in) in diameter, smell strongly of liquorice. This summer-flowering species requires warm house treatment, where it needs plenty of headroom and requires very little rest.

Coelogyne corymbosa

Attractive, pristine white flowers are produced in profusion on this modestly sized species from Darjeeling. The flower spikes arch low beneath the foliage, making it an ideal subject for basket culture. This high-altitude, cool-growing plant blooms in early summer.

Coelogyne asperata

Coelogyne cristata 'Glacier Mint'

Coelogyne cristata **var.** *alba*

Coelogyne cristata **var.** *alba*

The lovely, pure white form of the species has no colour adornment at all. The plant grows from a longer rhizome than the type, which results in a rather untidy appearance. It flowers in spring.

Coelogyne cristata **'Glacier Mint'**

Undoubtedly one of the most popular of the species suitable for the cool greenhouse or the indoor grower. Left to its own devices, the plants can become huge, resulting in a breathtaking display of brilliant white, 5cm (2in) flowers in early spring. It originates from the Himalayas.

Coelogyne flaccida

Coelogyne dayana

Coelogyne dayana

In summer, the downward-spiralling flower spike carries numerous 4cm (1½in) flowers, which are exquisitely marked in light and dark brown. The plant is tall and slender and needs to be grown in the intermediate greenhouse with good winter light. This species comes from Borneo.

Coelogyne flaccida

Masses of pendent flower spikes adorn this species. The 2.5cm (1in), ivory white blooms are fragrant and produced from the new growths in early summer. The plant is 20cm (8in) tall, and originates from the Khasi Hills in East India. Grow it indoors or in a cool greenhouse.

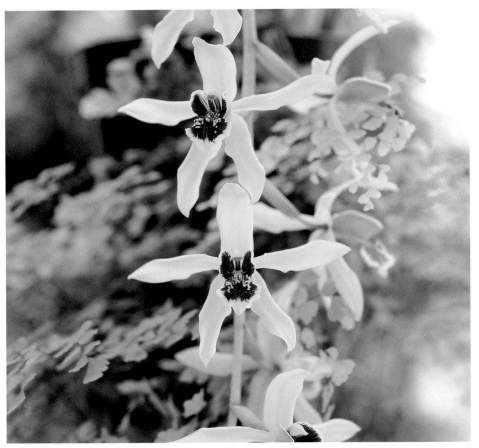

***Coelogyne* Green Dragon 'Chelsea' AM/RHS**

Coelogyne Green Dragon 'Chelsea' AM/RHS

This is one of the very few really good hybrids within this genus. The dramatic 7cm (3in) flowers have horizontally held green petals that contrast with the black lacing on the lip. The parents are *Coelogyne massangeana* and the apple green *C. pandurata*, which are both warm-growing species from Borneo. The hybrid blooms during the spring and summer.

Coelogyne Intermedia

This plant needs good light all year round and a dry period during the winter while it is resting. It blooms in the spring at the beginning of the growing season. The delicate, white flowers, on a drooping flower spike, last for three to four weeks.

Coelogyne lawrenceana

This species from South-east Asia produces its striking 6cm (2½in), yellow-green flowers on short sprays. The sepals are thin and ribbon-like, but the white lip is large and richly coloured at the centre. It is sequential-flowering, producing its blooms over a long period during summer.

Coelogyne Intermedia

Coelogyne lawrenceana

Coelogyne ochracea

Coelogyne Memoria William Micholitz 'Burnham' AM/RHS

A combination of the species *Coelogyne lawrenceana* and *C. mooreana* has resulted in this striking hybrid, which produces its flowers in succession from a long spike. The large blooms are pristine white with a deep golden lip, and appear in spring.

Coelogyne mooreana 'Brockhurst' FCC/RHS

Awarded in 1906, this species is represented by propagations of a single clone from an importation from Vietnam at that time. At 7cm (3in), the flowers are the largest of the white-flowered coelogynes, at their best when blooming in spring. Some hybridizing has been done with this cool-growing species.

Coelogyne ochracea

A compact growing species from Nepal with prettily marked, 2.5cm (1in), white flowers, yellow in the centre, which are produced on upright flower spikes above the pseudobulbs. The flowers are strongly scented and appear from the new growth in spring. Grow cool and rest in winter.

Coelogyne velutina

Long spikes of cream flowers, with brown streaked lips, tumble from the base of this robust Malayan species, which likes a warm greenhouse with good winter light. It produces a plant that is 60cm (2ft) tall and requires plenty of room to grow. It does well in a hanging basket.

Coelogyne Memoria William Micholitz 'Burnham' AM/RHS

Coelogyne mooreana 'Brockhurst' FCC/RHS

Coelogyne velutina

CYMBIDIUM

Species of *Cymbidium* are surprisingly few in number when one considers the tens of thousands of hybrids that have been raised over a period of 100 years. Of the 50 or so species widely distributed throughout Asia, it was hardly more than half a dozen from the Himalayan regions of India and Nepal that became the building blocks for the first hybrids. Those once considered to be the main species in this natural genus are *Cymbidium insigne, C. lowianum, C. eburneum* and *C. tracyanum,* all cultivated for their showy flowers. Once hybrids began to appear, the species became less attractive to growers, who were looking for improved shape and size. The species, once so plentiful, were often disposed of in favour of the new hybrids, until they were hardly represented in collections. Today there is renewed interest in these and other species, which are considered rare collectors' items, and the finest clones are much sought after.

For the beginner and amateur grower who is not looking to build up a specialist collection of these species, the modern hybrids represent a much better purchase. The hybrids come in a multitude of colours and sizes to suit all situations, and the flowers will last for months rather than weeks. While the first hybrids were all spring-flowering, further breeding lines developed later from alternative species such as *Cymbidium ensifolium, C. floribundum, C. devonianum* and *C. madidum,* with which the flowering season has been extended to cover most of the year. Some growers concentrate entirely on this one genus, finding that they are continually able to add variation to their collection because they never exceed the choice available.

Cymbidiums are tall-growing plants with several long, strap-like leaves and sheathed pseudobulbs. The plants can grow to 1m (3ft) tall, with flower spikes above the foliage on the standard varieties but shorter on the miniature types. The flower spikes, which are mostly staked upright, can become top heavy so they need to be supported to prevent them snapping under the weight of the buds. A dozen or more blooms are produced, some of which are delicately scented.

Cymbidiums need regular repotting to prevent them becoming overburdened with leafless pseudobulbs. These are the older, back bulbs that have shed their leaves but remain alive for a few more years, supporting the main plant. When there are more out of leaf than in leaf, the older back bulbs will become a drain on the plant and restrict its progress. These should be cut off at repotting time and can be propagated from if wished. Often, the main plant can return to the same size pot when its pseudobulbs are reduced in this way. Large plants can be divided, provided that each piece contains at least one new growth and three supporting pseudobulbs. Repot in the spring as soon as the plant has finished flowering. Cymbidiums grow throughout the year, but more slowly during the winter in balance with the shorter days and colder nights.

Cymbidiums are easily obtainable from various outlets when they are in flower, but beginners to orchid growing often find that they are unable to flower the plants again the following year. The most common cause of this is lack of light, particularly when the plants are being grown indoors. Placing them out of doors for the summer will ensure that the plants receive all the light they require and, as a result, will produce a fine display of blooms in their next season.

Cymbidium **Bethlehem 'Ridgeway'**

Do not allow the plants to stand in the direct midday sun, which will badly scorch their leaves. Give them a shady spot in the garden where they will catch the early morning or late evening sun.

Cymbidiums are grown the world over for the pot-plant trade, as well as for the cut-flower trade. Where they can be grown outdoors all year round, such as in California and parts of Australia, they represent a multi-million pound industry.

The original species from which the hybrids have come are evergreen epiphytic or terrestrial plants. Because of their large size, the hybrids are grown in pots.

Temperature: Cool-growing.

Cultivation: Grow in pots, at least 15cm (6in) in diameter, of coarse bark or Rockwool. Water and feed all year, but in winter allow the plants to dry out partially between waterings. Mist in summer. Keep in good light, but shade from direct sun in summer to prevent leaf scorch.

Height: To 1m (3ft).

Cymbidium Bethlehem 'Ridgeway'

This fine variety of a well-known hybrid is a free-flowering plant which needs plenty of light all year. The white flowers are tinged with pink, with dark pink spotting on the lip. They appear in winter, and will last for eight to ten weeks, produced from flower spikes which emerge from late summer onwards.

Cymbidium Bouley Bay

Bouley Bay, which flowers in winter and spring, is a modern hybrid of *Cymbidium lowianum*, the result of over 100 years of breeding. It retains the green colour.

Cymbidium Bulbarrow 'Will Stuckley' AM/RHS

This spring-flowering, yellow beauty, with its maroon lip, is a hybrid of the epiphyte *Cymbidium devonianum* from Darjeeling, and *C.* Weston Rose, which traces back to *C. insigne*. The size has increased from a 2.5cm (1in) bloom in one generation.

Cymbidium **Bouley Bay (left) and** *C. lowianum* **(right)**

Cymbidium devonianum **(left) and** *C.* **Bulbarrow 'Will Stuckley' AM/RHS (right)**

Cymbidium Cherry Blossom 'Profusion'

Cymbidium Cotil Point

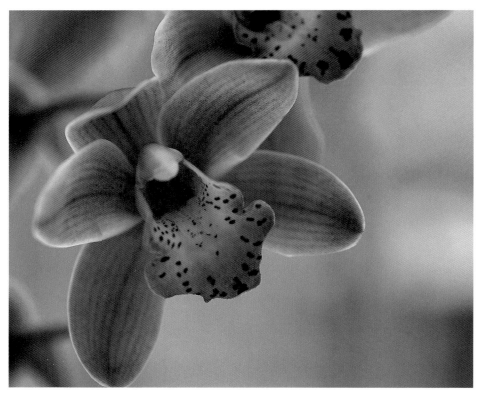

Cymbidium Embers 'Yowie Bay'

Cymbidium **Cherry Blossom 'Profusion'**
This is a miniature type achieved by crossing the species *Cymbidium erythrostylum* and *C. pumilum* (now reclassified as *C. floribundum*). The plant will reach flowering size in a 10–13cm (4–5in) pot with flower spikes 25cm (10in) long. The flowers, which are pale pink with a lip heavily spotted with darker pink, appear in winter.

Cymbidium **Cotil Point**
This fine modern hybrid, which flowers in spring, has a perfect shape and colouring. The rich pink has been brought forward from *Cymbidium insigne*.

Cymbidium **Embers 'Yowie Bay'**
This is a named variety of a popular hybrid which can be grown indoors in good light or placed out of doors for the summer growing season. The blooms, produced in winter, will last for eight to ten weeks. Water the plant all year.

Cymbidium erythrostylum

Cymbidium insigne 'Mrs Carl Holmes'

Cymbidium erythrostylum

This delightful species from Vietnam holds its lateral petals thrust forward to hug the lip. Its perfect, pristine-white blooms, which appear in autumn and winter, have produced some excellent hybrids.

Cymbidium insigne 'Mrs Carl Holmes'

Vietnam and China are the home of this tall-growing species. It grows terrestrially and produces flower spikes of up to 1.5m (5ft) long. The flowers are extremely long-lasting and vary from dark pink to white. The flowers appear in spring.

Cymbidium Jocelyn

The flowers of this *Cymbidium* hybrid will last for eight to ten weeks during the winter. The pink petals and sepals are veined, and the cream and yellow lips are blotched and edged with red. The plant should be kept in a cool position, especially at night, while it is in bloom and placed out of doors for the summer growing season.

Cymbidium Jocelyn

Cymbidium **Lady McAlpine**

Cymbidium Lady McAlpine

The white flowers of this spring-flowering orchid have been influenced by the species *Cymbidium eburneum*, which, when crossed with *C. lowianum*, gives the red lip. This is a large-growing, standard-type hybrid that begs a grand setting.

Cymbidium Loch Lomond

This beautiful, modern hybrid, which flowers in winter, can trace its ancestry back to *Cymbidium lowianum*. The large green petals and china-white lip with a red horseshoe are characteristic of this line of breeding.

Cymbidium Maureen Grapes 'Marilyn'

This summer-flowering, highly fragrant variety produces its flower spikes in succession. As one finishes, the next buds are just opening; this greatly extends the flowering season through several months.

Cymbidium **Loch Lomond**

Cymbidium **Maureen Grapes 'Marilyn'**

Cymbidium **Mavourneen 'Jester' AM/RHS**
In this unusual, spring-flowering hybrid, the pink lip patterning is repeated on the petals, giving the appearance of a flower with three lips. This is called peloric marking, and becomes unstable when introduced into hybridizing.

Cymbidium **Mini Ice 'Antarctic'**
Where space is limited, this smaller-growing hybrid is ideal and will provide an abundance of green flowers, with deep red-spotted lips, during early spring. Water all year, and apply feed for most of the year.

Cymbidium **Nevada**
This specimen plant with its multiple flower spikes requires a large setting. The spikes are 1.5m (5ft) tall and the brilliant, golden yellow, non-fading flowers are 13cm (5in) across.

Cymbidium Mini Ice 'Antarctic'

Cymbidium Mavourneen 'Jester' AM/RHS

Cymbidium Nevada

Cymbidium **Pontiac**

An excellent modern, red hybrid with 10–12cm (4–5in) blooms which are carried on long flower spikes in the spring. It retains some signs of its origins from the species *Cymbidium tracyanum*, which is revealed by the stripes on the petals and by the beautiful lip patterning.

Cymbidium **Sarah Jean 'Ice Cascade'**

This is a first generation hybrid from *Cymbidium pumilum*. It has small, white flowers with yellow centres in spring. The flowers measure 5cm (2in) across and grow on pendent flower spikes.

Cymbidium **Sarah Jean 'Icicle'**

This spring-flowering hybrid, with its profusion of delicate, white flowers, will enhance any situation. Keep the plant well watered throughout the year, but avoid overwetting in winter. Place in a cool room away from any source of heat or draughts.

Cymbidium Pontiac

Cymbidium Sarah Jean 'Ice Cascade'

Cymbidium Sarah Jean 'Icicle'

Cymbidium **Scott's Sunrise 'Aurora'**
Orange is a colour not generally
associated with cymbidiums, but this
winter-flowering hybrid, with its red-
edged lip, is coming close to a new
colour breakthrough.

Cymbidium **Summer Pearl 'Senna'**
The erect flower spikes of greenish yellow
flowers, with lips that are heavily
spotted with maroon, appear between
spring and autumn.

Cymbidium **Summer Pearl 'Sonia'**
Between spring and late summer, this
lovely orchid produces erect spikes of
creamy pink flowers, with lips heavily
spotted with maroon.

Cymbidium tracyanum
A late summer-flowering species from
Burma and Thailand, this strong-growing
plant has large blooms. There are many
hidden colours in this flower, but it has
mainly contributed its red to hybrids.

Cymbidium Summer Pearl 'Sonia'   *Cymbidium* Summer Pearl 'Senna'

Cymbidium Scott's Sunrise 'Aurora'   *Cymbidium tracyanum*

DENDROBIUM

This is an extremely large and varied natural genus containing both deciduous and evergreen types, which are widely distributed throughout India and China, and through the Malaysian peninsula to New Guinea, Australia and New Zealand. Of the 900 or so species, nearly all are epiphytic. Vast numbers of species are in cultivation, in addition to many hybrids. For the hobby grower, the hybrids are mainly confined to the Indian species, and a wonderfully decorative range has been developed using *Dendrobium nobile* as a starting point. With the additional use of related species, hybrids have been produced in a rainbow of colours, with the beautifully rounded blooms amassed on the plant in spring. While hybridizing has been carried out with other distinct groups, only this one has achieved the pinnacle of success associated with the *D. nobile* hybrids.

Dendrobium bigibbum from northern Australia has been responsible for an astonishing variety of hybrids within its group. Numerous varieties are available, with flowers that range from powdery white, through clear yellow, green and pink to the deepest purple and mauve. Unlike the *D. nobile* types, these can be used for the cut-flower trade and are bred extensively and exclusively for this purpose. The cut blooms from plants grown in the tropical conditions of South-east Asia, as well as their native Australia, are flown around the world for sale in florists and other outlets.

Dendrobiums will not all interbreed with each other. Among the several distinct groups that are identified, only those that are closely related will hybridize. The evergreen varieties from Papua New Guinea, such as *Dendrobium canaliculatum*, for example, are incompatible with the Indian species, such as *D. densiflorum*. Between the different divisions within the genus are species that bear little resemblance to one another. The amazing variety of form, shape and colour is one of the fascinating attractions of this genus. Hybrids apart, the diversity is huge.

Typically, dendrobiums produce short to tall pseudobulbs, which can be extremely long and thin, becoming drooping as they grow, or stout and rigidly upright. They may be leafed along their entire length, the narrowly oval, thinly textured leaves appearing diagonally, as in *Dendrobium pierardii*. Among the evergreen species, one of the most popular is *D. bigibbum*. This species has upright stems leafed to about halfway, and the foliage is more heavily textured. There are extremes, such as *D. cuthbertsonii* from New Guinea, which has short, squat pseudobulbs and a single leaf. Among the deciduous types, including *D. nobile*, which becomes evergreen under cultivation, the flowers are produced in ones and twos from nodes that appear opposite the leaf bases. The large, rounded blooms are held on short stems. *D. densiflorum* and others produce a few, roundly oval, heavily textured leaves from the top portion of the squarish pseudobulbs, the blooms hanging on a dense, clustered truss. Most of the Indonesian and Australian species carry their highly specialised blooms on long sprays with up to a dozen flowers.

Dendrobium cuthbertsonii

Most dendrobiums have well-defined growing and resting periods, with new growth starting in spring at the same time as the buds are forming. They produce their growth rapidly during summer, completing it by autumn. Because most are tall-growing plants, there is a tendency to overpot. Some require more specialist culture to ensure a good flowering.

Dendrobium brymerianum

Dendrobium delicatum

Temperature: Cool- to intermediate-growing.
Cultivation: Grow in pots that restrict the roots, in bark compost (growing medium). For anchorage, weigh down the base of the pot with stones or set in a heavier container. Those with long, drooping canes can be grown epiphytically on bark. Allow good light, shading in summer only to prevent leaf scorch. Start watering gradually as soon as new growth appears in spring. Water plants of the *Dendrobium nobile* group very sparingly until the flower buds are defined, or these will develop as adventitious growths rather than as flowers. Water and feed liberally as growth speeds up. Keep all dendrobiums dry in winter.
Height: 15–45cm (6–18in).

Dendrobium brymerianum

An extremely rare, early spring-flowering species not often seen in cultivation, this orchid is a challenge to grow well. Its deep golden yellow flowers are extraordinary for the deeply fringed, or bearded, lip. The plant is tall and slender and comes from Burma and Thailand, but is no longer imported from the wild.

Dendrobium cuthbertsonii

Among the most concise of the genus, this diminutive, spring-flowering species with short, clustered stems produces comparatively large (2cm/¾in) flowers, variously coloured pink to red, singly from the top of the cane. Rapidly gaining in popularity, the species comes from New Guinea.

Dendrobium delicatum

Long sprays of highly fragrant, densely packed, small, creamy white flowers festoon this tough, hard-caned *Dendrobium* in spring. It is at its best when allowed to grow on into a specimen plant.

Dendrobium fimbriatum **var.** *oculatum*

Dendrobium fimbriatum var. *oculatum*

This golden yellow species from India produces its flowers in spring on loose pendent trusses from the top portion of the slender, leafless canes. The deep, almost black "eye" at the centre of the lip makes a striking contrast. This once plentiful species is now considered quite rare.

Dendrobium Gatton Sunray FCC/RHS

This very old hybrid was awarded around the turn of the 20th century. The plant grows extremely tall, to 1.2m (4ft), and the large 10cm (4in) flowers are produced in early summer in loose trusses from the top part of the canes. The striking flowers are a combination of corn yellow with a deep maroon centre to the lip.

Dendrobium infundibulum

A native of India and Thailand, this lovely crystalline, white-flowered species produces its large 8cm (3in) blooms in abundance from the top portion of the black-haired, or hirsute, cane in the spring. It is an easy and rewarding species for the beginner.

Dendrobium Gatton Sunray FCC/RHS

Dendrobium infundibulum

Dendrobium kingianum

Dendrobium kingianum

A hard-caned Australian species that is of compact size, this blooms with a profusion of small 3cm (1¼in) flowers on spikes held above the foliage. The plant will grow indoors or in a cool greenhouse where it likes plenty of good light. Flowering occurs in autumn and also at other times.

Dendrobium miyakei

This rather untidy looking species from the Philippines produces its flowers in pompons along the leafless canes. The flowers are striped mauve and appear throughout the summer at various times. The plant should be grown fairly warm with good light. If the plant is grown in a basket, the canes will droop.

Dendrobium New Comet 'Red Queen'

This is one of the best examples of the breeding qualities of *Dendrobium nobile*, which has helped to produce this hybrid with its deep mauve flowers with maroon lips. The plant flowers along the whole length of the soft canes in early spring.

Dendrobium miyakei

Dendrobium **New Comet 'Red Queen'**

Dendrobium **Seigyoku 'Queen'**

Dendrobium New Guinea

New Guinea is the home to some of the most extraordinary species in this genus, and this New Guinea hybrid is one of only a few worthwhile hybrids to have emerged from this group. The nodding, deep yellow flowers are produced in spring and summer on loose trusses from the top of the hard, two-leafed canes. The flowers will last for many months in perfect condition.

Dendrobium Seigyoku 'Queen'

This lovely red-and-white *Dendrobium nobile*-type hybrid, which flowers in spring, was raised in Japan. The flowers appear in profusion on short stems.

Dendrobium victoria-regina

The attractive mauve-tinted flowers are produced in small clusters in spring from the older, leafless canes on this species from the Philippines. The warm-growing plant is deciduous in cultivation and needs a good rest in winter.

Dendrobium **New Guinea**

Dendrobium victoria-regina

ENCYCLIA

There are about 150 species in this easily recognizable genus, of which a great many have flowers with the lip uppermost. Many are small- or compact-growing plants that will grow into good-sized specimens. All are evergreen, epiphytic plants and most originate from Mexico. While the species are extremely popular and widely grown, there has been very little hybridizing within the genus. Some species have been used with excellent results when crossed with cattleyas or other related genera. When used for hybridizing, the genus is referred to as *Epidendrum*. Hence, a cross between *Encyclia* and *Cattleya* produces *Epicattleya*.

While the dominant colours within the genus are pale, often whitish, these flowers carry a strong fragrance. Especially lovely are *Encyclia radiata* and *E. lancifolia*. These, and others, produce good-looking plants with shiny, elongated pseudobulbs and a pair of mid-green leaves. The flowers come on short to medium, upright flower spikes between the leaves. Distinctly different is *E. vitellina* – the only species with bright vermillion flowers – which has a bluish bloom on its foliage. Further species, such as *E. nemorale*, produce hard, rounded pseudobulbs with long, stiffened leaves; their flowers are held on long spikes and their lips are at the base of the flowers. The plants bloom from spring to midsummer, and last for several weeks.

Encyclias make attractive plants for growing indoors. They are also ideal for the beginner, producing their flowers freely in their season. Most have a decided rest in the winter. A mixed collection should contain at least a few of these endearing orchids.

Temperature: Cool-growing.

Cultivation: Grow in pots or baskets of bark-based compost (growing medium). Water freely, when in active growth, and spray overhead, except when in flower. Keep shaded in summer, although those

Encyclia adenocaula

Encyclia brassavolae

Encyclia cochleata **var. 'Yellow Burnham'**

with hard, rounded pseudobulbs will tolerate more light. In winter, water just enough to keep the pseudobulbs plump. *Height*: 7–30cm (3–12in).

Encyclia adenocaula

This hard-bulbed type, which comes from Mexico, produces a long flower spike from the top of the rounded pseudobulb in spring and early summer. The mauve flowers have a red-and-white lip. Grow in a cool greenhouse in good light and rest in winter.

Encyclia brassavolae

This handsome species produces tall, slender pseudobulbs. The 5cm (2in), narrow-petalled, green flowers, which are carried on an upright spike, have a white, heart-shaped lip, of which the tip is dipped in rosy mauve. The plant is summer-flowering.

Encyclia lancifolia

Encyclia cochleata var. 'Yellow Burnham'

An extremely popular orchid which does well indoors and which can grow into a large plant over 30cm (12in) high. The flower spikes, with their green flowers with orange-yellow lips, are much taller, and will remain in bloom on mature plants for many months at various times of the year.

Encyclia lancifolia

This neat orchid, 15cm (6in) tall, produces upright flower spikes in summer. The 3cm (1¼in) blooms are starry and ivory-white, with a red-lined lip which is held uppermost. This is a particularly easy and delightful species to grow indoors or in a cool greenhouse.

Encyclia polybulbon

This dwarf plant with clustered pseudobulbs supports two leaves. The single 2cm (¾in) flowers come from between the leaves and cover the plant with their star-like presence. Narrow, light tawny-brown petals and sepals are set off by the large white lip. This cool-growing species flowers in early summer.

Encyclia radiata

An attractive and fragrant species from Guatemala, this makes good-looking plants, 23cm (9in) tall, that bloom freely in the summer. The flower spikes are held upright above the foliage and, like many in this genus, hold their red-lined lip at the top of the flower.

Encyclia vitellina

Of all the species in the *Encyclia* genus, this is unique for its rich orange-red colouring. The plant produces a tall, often branching, flower spike in autumn as the season's pseudobulb is completed. The plant comes from Mexico and Guatemala.

Encyclia polybulbon

Encyclia radiata

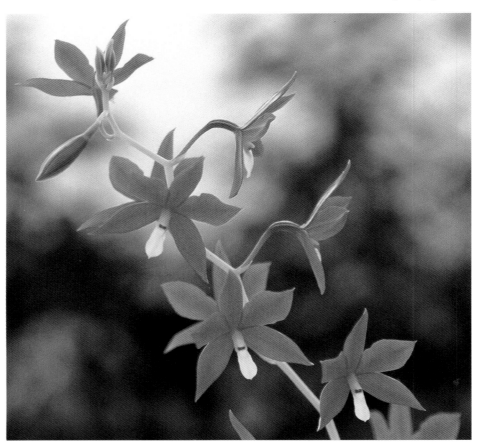

Encyclia vitellina

EPIDENDRUM

Epidendrums come in an extremely varied range of sizes, from small tufted plants of less than 15cm (6in) high with clustered, leafy stems (such as *Epidendrum porpax*), to the tall, reedy-stemmed giants of *E. revolutum* and *E. ibaquense*. The latter can attain a height of over 2m (6½ft). In between these extremes are a number of attractive plants with pseudobulbs, including *E. ciliare*, which more closely resemble the encyclias to which they are closely related and with which they were at one time combined.

Widely distributed throughout tropical America, this is a huge genus containing hundreds of species, some of them extremely similar in appearance. Of these, a good number are grown, and there are a few hybrids that are worth looking out for.

Epidendrums are evergreen epiphytic or terrestrial, and sometimes lithophytic, plants with widely varying flowers whose colours range through white, green, brown, pink and red. As a genus it is difficult to get to know, because there are so many distinctly different plants, but this makes their study more interesting. Some of the taller-growing species produce large heads of flowers which, on a large plant, become perpetually flowering, as does *Epidendrum radicans*. Members of this diverse group produce their flowers at different times, but will give a good show during the summer.
Temperature: Cool- to intermediate-growing.
Cultivation: Grow reed-types in 10–15cm (4–6in) pots or prepared beds of coarse bark and sand or peat (or an alternative), and leave undisturbed. Water throughout the year. Grow small, creeping types in small baskets or on bark supports. Water freely when in active growth, and less in winter, when overwatering can cause rotting.
Height: 15–200cm (6–78in).

Epidendrum Burtonii
This is an old-time hybrid from the species *Epidendrum radicans*, which it resembles. Note the extending flower spike where earlier orange blooms have been and the further buds developing at the tip. The flowers can appear at any time.

Epidendrum Burtonii

Epidendrum Plastic Doll
This is one of a very few hybrids developed from the *Epidendrum pseudepidendrum*. The flowers have green petals and sepals set off by a yellow, frilly lip. Several flowers are carried on the flower spike well above the foliage. Grow this plant in the intermediate to warm greenhouse where there is sufficient headroom.

Epidendrum Plastic Doll

Epidendrum pseudepidendum var. *album*

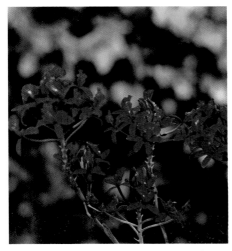

Epidendrum radicans

Epidendrum radicans

Tall, branching stems that produce aerial roots freely along their length typify this species which flowers at any time of the year. Its red flowers have their lip at the top of the flower and are borne on ever-growing flower spikes, which are an extension of the stems; a large plant becomes perpetually blooming.

Epidendrum radicans var. *alba*

In this white form of the species from Mexico, the flowers lack the bright red pigmentation. The plants are usually smaller growing, but bloom freely all year round.

Epidendrum pseudepidendrum

Epidendrum pseudepidendrum

This orchid has tall, slender, leafy stems, at the top of which several striking flowers are carried loosely in spring and summer. These have deep green petals and sepals, with a distinctive orange lip protruding from the rest of the flower. A native of Costa Rica, this is best grown in intermediate conditions.

Epidendrum pseudepidendrum var. *album*

This is a paler form of the type which lacks the bright contrast between the pink lip and the yellow petals and sepals. Its paler colouring is nevertheless most attractive, and the flowers are produced in spring and summer on larger clusters at the top of the stem.

Epidendrum radicans var. *alba*

LAELIA

There are about 50 species of *Laelia*, which are found throughout Central and South America, with a high concentration in Mexico. They divide into several distinct groups depending upon their habits, which vary considerably. All the species are lovely and extremely showy, but many had been difficult to find in cultivation until recent breeding programmes increased the availability of some of the finest types, such as the fabulous varieties of *L. purpurata* from Brazil. The genus is closely related to *Cattleya*, and the plants are sometimes difficult to tell apart. From the early days of hybridizing, laelias were crossed with cattleyas to such an extent that there are more laeliocattleyas than interspecific hybrids.

Laelias are evergreen epiphytic plants, their size varying from 15cm (6in) to 1m (3ft) tall. A number of the smaller growing species have petite, brightly coloured flowers held on upright sprays above the foliage. These plants, such as *Laelia cinnabarina*, produce slender pseudobulbs with a single, semi-rigid leaf. The larger types, such as *L. crispa*, resemble cattleyas, while others, which include *L. anceps*, are more distinct with squarish pseudobulbs and a shiny single leaf. Their flowers are carried on tall, slender flower spikes, at the end of which the large, 10cm (4in) blooms are held in a loose cluster. Many of the species bloom in the autumn, while others produce their flowers in the spring at the beginning of the growing season.

Beginners could not do better than to include such beauties as *Laelia anceps* and *L. gouldiana* in their first collections. These plants are good, robust growers that grow with amazing ease and form large, clustered plants within a few years. The small-growing plants such as *L. flava* and *L. cinnabarina* need more specialist care because their pseudobulbs can easily shrivel and the plants quickly dehydrate as a result.

Temperature: Intermediate-growing (cool-growing for Mexican species).

Cultivation: Grow in 10cm (4in) pots of bark compost (growing medium). The smaller species can also be grown on bark. Water well during the summer but allow them almost to dry out in winter when resting. Give some shade in summer and full light in winter.

Height: 15–100cm (6–36in).

Laelia anceps

This delightful, cool-growing species can be grown indoors or in a greenhouse. The flower spikes can grow to a height of 60cm (2ft). The mauve flowers, which are large and variable in appearance, have yellow-centred, deep pink lips and appear in early autumn. The plant comes originally from Mexico.

Laelia anceps

Laelia anceps '**Guerrero**'

Laelia anceps var. alba

The white form of the species is just as attractive as its coloured form, and has been used to hybridize, retaining the pure colour. The flower spikes are usually shorter than in the type.

Laelia anceps 'Guerrero'

This named variety of the species, which flowers in autumn, is unusual for its exceptionally deep coloured lip. It has been selected for breeding hybrids, some of which retain the rich colouring. There are several further lovely and distinct varietal clones of this species in cultivation.

Laelia milleri × L. briegeri

This primary hybrid was achieved by crossing two of the smaller-flowered species. These compact plants have neat pseudobulbs and golden yellow flowers on an upright flower spike that appears from the top of the pseudobulb in the summer. Grow in an intermediate greenhouse.

Laelia anceps var. *alba*

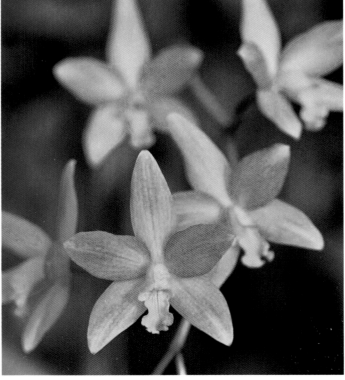

Laelia milleri × *L. briegeri*

Laelia purpurata var. *alba*

Laelia purpurata

This lovely species from Brazil grows extremely well in the intermediate greenhouse. It produces slender pseudobulbs and carries several 10cm (4in), white flowers with a purple lip on a stem during the spring and summer months.

Laelia purpurata var. *alba*

There are many examples of albino, or white, forms of species among laelias and cattleyas. This summer-flowering Brazilian species has many named varietal forms, which have been maintained by raising from seed in cultivation.

Laelia purpurata var. *carnea*

This extremely handsome species resembles the *Cattleya* family in appearance and has been used extensively to produce *Laeliocattleya* hybrids. This summer-flowering variety is unusual because of its salmon-coloured lip.

Laelia purpurata var. *carnea*

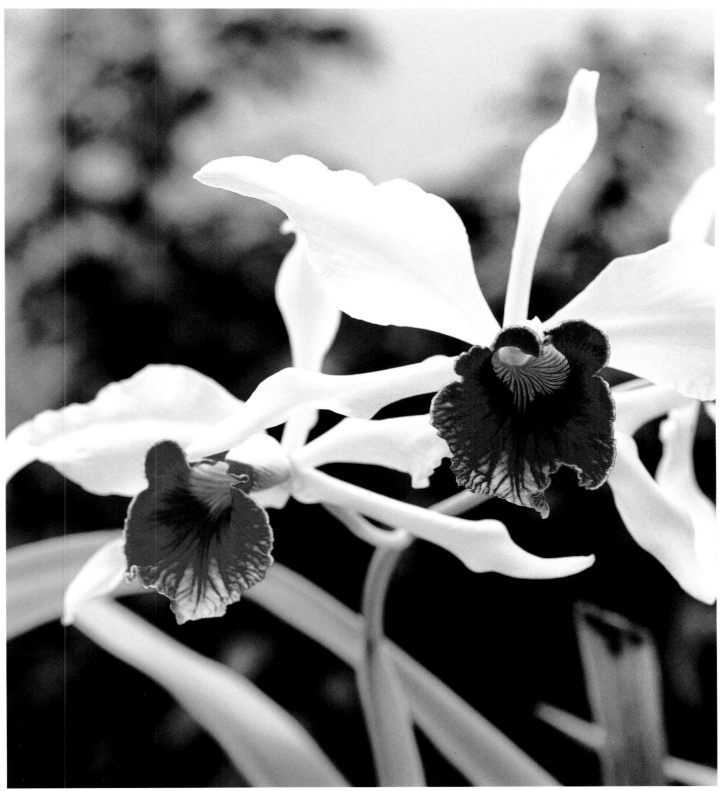

Laelia purpurata

LYCASTE ALLIANCE

The lycastes are a relatively small, but influential, natural genus of medium-size plants. They have had a great impact on the related anguloas with which they will readily interbreed to produce some of the most showy artificial hybrids. The majority of the flowers are typically triangular, the shape formed by the widely spread sepals that frame the cupped petals and lip. When crossed with the tulip-shaped anguloas, the superb, large, open-flowered angulocastes are produced, which have done much to promote this alliance. Although the majority of the species within the lycastes and anguloas are of pale colouring, the rosy-red varieties of *Lycaste skinneri* have emphasized rich colours in hybrids such as *L.* Wyld Fire. In the same way, dark red angulocastes have been raised that compare well with the lighter, softer-coloured varieties.

The strongest fragrance in these genera is found among the *Anguloa* species, and this has carried on into the bigeneric hybrids. *A. clowesii* is best known for its sweet perfume.

The lycastes and anguloas share many characteristics. They produce stout, hard, dark green pseudobulbs that are generously foliaged during the summer. The leaves are broad, soft and ribbed, spreading wide as they mature, which makes the plants space-consuming. The foliage is shed during winter or at the onset of new growth in early spring. As the leaves mature, they become spotted and yellowed with age; it is often best to remove them before they drop naturally. The plants have a decided winter's rest. New growth is seen in early spring, and the new shoots are accompanied by numerous, single-flowered spikes, clustering around the base of the pseudobulb. They grow quickly and the flowers appear before being swamped by the spreading foliage. The plants grow rapidly during the summer, producing their large pseudobulbs, 7–15cm (3–6in) high, before winter.

Annual repotting is often preferred for lycastes and anguloas because the plants quickly outgrow their containers. By removing the oldest pseudobulbs each time, plants can be kept to a moderate size. Where specimen plants are wanted, you can leave them to become really large. For these reasons, the hybrids are best contained in a greenhouse where they can be given sufficient headroom.

If you are growing your orchids indoors where space is limited, try one or two of the smaller species among the lycastes such as *Lycaste aromatica*, which is deliciously scented and carries a profusion of golden yellow flowers in the spring, or *L. skinneri*, with its variable white to soft pink varieties. These plants will not grow much bigger than 30cm (12in) high when in leaf.

Most of the 25 or so *Lycaste* species can be found in cultivation, alongside the numerous hybrids. The species may be epiphytic, terrestrial or lithophytic, with most plants preferring shady situations in woodland.

Lycastes are South American orchids whose highest concentrations are in Mexico and Peru. The anguloas are a small natural genus containing about ten species, which exist mainly in Colombia, Ecuador and Peru. Because of their scarcity, only a few species are widely grown. More widely seen in orchid collections are the angulocastes, whose large, fleshy blooms are 10cm (4in) wide.

Temperature: Cool-growing (winter) and intermediate-growing (summer).

Cultivation: Grow in pots of bark-based compost (growing medium) in pots up to 25cm (10in) in diameter. In summer, water and feed freely and maintain good humidity (although excessive spraying can cause leaf marks). Decrease watering as the foliage begins to turn yellow, and water in winter only if the pseudobulbs become dehydrated and shrivel. Give light shade in summer and full light in winter.

Height: 30cm–1m (12–36in).

Anguloa virginalis

Anguloa clowesii

Anguloa clowesii

A most handsome, large-growing, cool-house orchid, this early summer-flowering species has leaves that reach 1m (3ft) tall when mature. The deep yellow flowers, which appear in early summer, are strongly scented, and the rocking lip gives rise to its common name of cradle orchid.

Anguloa virginalis

A single, pale pink, fragrant flower appears in early summer on each spike held below the developing foliage. The sepals and petals remain cupped, not opening fully, as is typical of flowers in this genus.

Angulocaste Jupiter AM/RHS

This older, spring-flowering hybrid retains its youthful looks with densely spotted sepals overlying a light yellow base. This bigeneric hybrid is between *Lycaste* and *Anguloa*.

Lycaste aromatica

This pretty, scented species from South America produces an abundance of golden yellow flowers in spring. The plant is deciduous and rests during the winter. Note the new growth just starting.

Augulocaste **Jupiter AM/RHS**

Lycaste aromatica

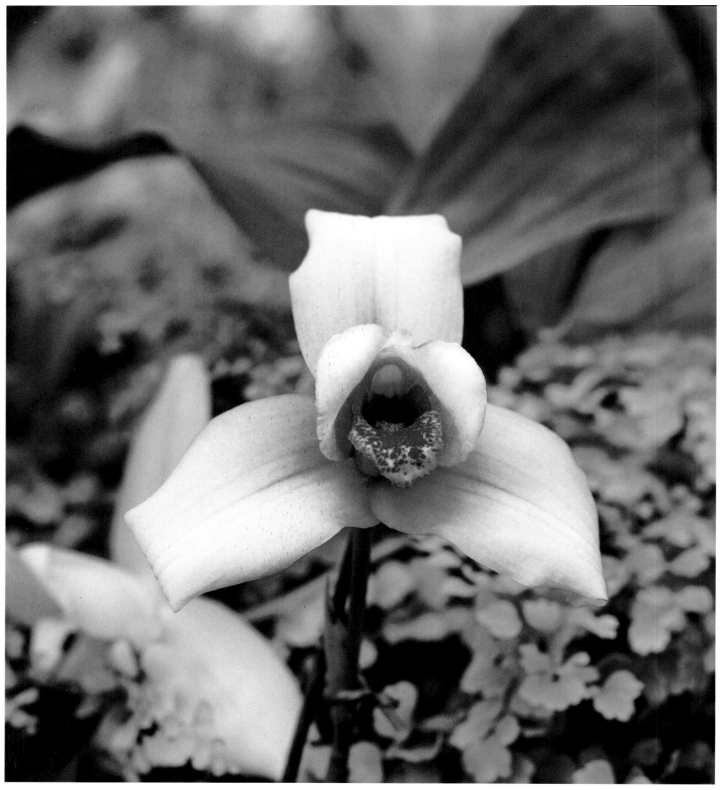

Lycaste skinneri

Lycaste Autumn Glow

With strong, brown sepals contrasting with
the deep yellow petals and lip, this lovely
autumn-flowering, cool-growing hybrid
reflects the season well. The plant will rest
after flowering.

Lycaste skinneri

A variable species from Guatemala, this
is typical of the lycastes with their three-
cornered flowers, where the pale pink
sepals stand away from the petals that hug
the brightly coloured lip. Single flowers,
7cm (3in) wide, are produced in spring on
stems that are shorter than the foliage on
this deciduous plant.

Lycaste Wyld Surprise

This is one of a range of beautiful hybrids
that have been raised using *Lycaste skinneri*
as a starting point. Single-flowered stems
surround the pseudobulbs at the same
time as the new growths are appearing.
This lovely, reddish-pink grex is a stunning
example of the variation in rich colourings
that can be achieved from one cross, where
each clone will be unique. The flowers
appear in spring.

Lycaste Autumn Glow

Lycaste Wyld Surprise

MASDEVALLIA

Affectionately known as kite orchids for the long "tails" of some of the flowers in this vast natural genus, the masdevallias are small- to medium-size plants that have single-leafed, short stems on a creeping rhizome. The leaves are oval to long, and mid- to dark green in colour. The slender flower spikes come from the base and may be single-flowered or have several on a stem. The flowers are very variable in shape and colour. While some species, such as *Masdevallia coccinea*, produce some of the most vibrant colours in the orchid flora, others are very drab. Of the 300 or so species, many are in cultivation alongside a small number of hybrids.

The flowers are characterized by the triangular shape of the large, spreading sepals, of which some (such as those of *Masdevallia caudata*) have extended "tails". The petals and lip are much reduced and remain generally hidden at the centre of the bloom. In other species, such as *M. racemosa*, the sepals are fused at the base to create a tube that contains the diminutive other segments. While *M. veitchiana* is outstanding for its vibrant orange and red colouring, others, such as *M. ventricularia*, which has curious brown-spotted, tubular flowers, are nonetheless interesting and worth considering. The largest flower in the genus is that of *M. macrura*, which measures 30cm (12in) or more vertically from top to bottom. This impressive length arises because of the long, tapering sepals.

These evergreen epiphytic, or occasionally lithophytic, orchids inhabit cool, shady and moist areas of forest woodland high in the Andes of South America. In cultivation, they should be disturbed as little as possible, and, when repotting becomes necessary, they can often be "dropped on" into a slightly larger pot without breaking up the root ball. In this way, most masdevallias can be grown on to form good-size clumps without becoming unmanageable. At this stage they are seen at their best and will provide a profusion of flowers during the summer months. A few species, such as *Masdevallia tovarensis*, will produce more of its milk-white flowers from the same stems for more than one year, provided you do not cut them off.

Masdevallias are one natural genus which, in the past, has been combined with a huge number of related genera, including some unusual orchids, among them *Dryadella*, *Dracula*, *Trisetella* and *Pleurothallis*. The latter belongs to another vast group of related plants, which forms one of the largest natural genera with some 900 species. These produce flowers that vary from small to minuscule, where the only way to see them clearly is to view them through a magnifying glass.
Temperature: Cool-growing.
Cultivation: Grow in fine bark in plastic mesh pots of the type used for aquatic plants. Keep in shade year-round. Water carefully throughout the year, never allowing the roots to dry out, but also avoiding overwet conditions, which can lead to rotting.
Height: 15–30cm (6–12in).

Masdevallia coccinea
This elegant, tall-stemmed species carries its single, 5cm (2in), moon-shaped flowers high above the foliage. The bright purple of the spreading sepals is among the richest seen in any orchid flower. The plants bloom mainly throughout the spring and summer.

Masdevallia Falcon Sunrise
Three clones of this new hybrid have combined the qualities of several species to give exciting, orange flowers on medium-length stems. When grown on into specimen plants, these orchids will produce numerous flowers at various times of the year.

Masdevallia coccinea

Masdevallia **Falcon Sunrise**

Masdevallia Rose Mary
Among the many delightful hybrids that are gaining popularity among the masdevallias is this pretty, short-stemmed, pink-flowered variety. The flowers carry "tails" that adorn the sepals and appear at various times of the year.

Masdevallia Rose Mary

Masdevallia tovarensis

This delightful species comes from Venezuela and is a neat grower with 2.5cm (1in), white flowers which rise above the foliage. The flowers are produced at various times of the year. Each stem produces several flowers and will bloom again the following year, which is an unusual feature among masdevallias.

Masdevallia Whiskers

This tufted plant will produce numerous flowers in succession throughout the summer. The orange flowers stand clear of the foliage and have intensified coloration at the centre of the large, cupped sepals.

Masdevallia tovarensis

Masdevallia **Whiskers**

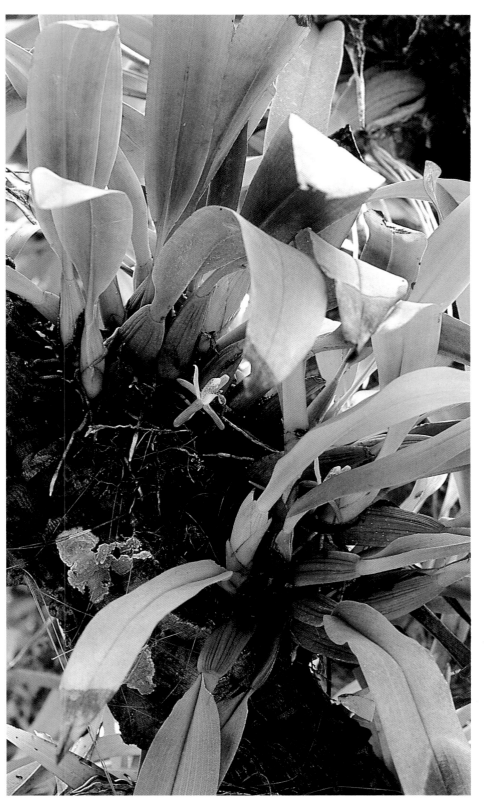

Maxillaria rufescens

MAXILLARIA

Inhabiting vast regions of Central and South America are the 300 or so evergreen, epiphytic or lithophytic species of *Maxillaria*. These are small- to medium-size plants that vary greatly in structure. The majority produce pseudobulbs, which may be small and round, with a single, grass-like leaf (such as *Maxillaria tenuifolia*), or large and spectacular (such as *M. sanderiana*). The latter, with its fleshy white, red-spotted flowers and triangular shape, resembles *Lycaste*, a genus into which most maxillarias were originally placed. Many of the species, and a very few hybrids, are grown. Of these, a number are often incorrectly named due to the similarity of some plants, which often cannot be told apart until they bloom.

Any number of the smaller-growing species are ideal beginners' orchids. They have a great willingness to grow and flower under extreme conditions and are more tolerant of a hot, dry environment than many other orchids. Those with the showiest flowers should be searched out; among these can be counted *Maxillaria picta*, which has deliciously fragrant blooms produced in abundance in autumn. Maxillarias bloom from the base, with a single flower on short to medium stems. The colours are variable, with yellow, buff-brown and red being the most frequent.

Most maxillarias prefer to be grown on, rather than continually divided into smaller pieces, when the limited number of flowers does not do justice to the plant when seen in its prime.

Temperature: Mainly cool-growing.

Cultivation: Grow in pots, larger varieties in coarse bark, smaller ones in fine bark. Those with a creeping rhizome can be grown in baskets or on bark. Keep in good light. Feed and water freely during summer, but give less in winter, without allowing the plants to dry out completely.

Height: 15–30cm (6–12in).

Maxillaria acutipetala

Maxillaria acutipetala

In summer, this pretty, distinctive species has pure yellow flowers with darker, reddish lips. The flowers are 2cm (¾in) across on stems less than 15cm (6in) high. This species is less often seen in collections and is rather rare.

Maxillaria coccinea

Unusually bright red colouring enhances these small, 2cm (¾in) wide, single flowers on thin, clustered stems well below the foliage. This is an easily grown, summer-flowering plant for the cool greenhouse or a shady position indoors.

Maxillaria luteo-alba

These 4cm (1½in) wide, cream flowers, with orange-brown sepals and yellow petals, are produced in early summer around the base of the leading pseudobulbs on 13cm (5in) stems, well below the foliage. This free-flowering, cool-growing species comes from Costa Rica and elsewhere.

Maxillaria ochroleuca

A spidery mass of fragrant flowers surrounds the base of this modestly sized, cool-growing plant from Honduras. The creamy white, spring flowers have either yellow or orange-red lips.

Maxillaria coccinea

Maxillaria luteo-alba

Maxillaria praestans

Presenting a uniform face, these alert brownish flowers with their almost black lips will last for several weeks during the summer months. The larger the plant, the more flowers it can be expected to produce.

Maxillaria tenuifolia

This gem produces long, straggly plants with pseudobulbs spaced along an upward-creeping rhizome. The single flowers, which appear in summer, are on short stems, with never more than one or two from one pseudobulb. The flowers are yellow, densely or lightly peppered with red, and fragrant.

Maxillaria ochroleuca

Maxillaria praestans

Maxillaria tenuifolia

MILTONIOPSIS

These orchids are without par in the orchid flora. They are the much-loved pansy orchids, so called because of their likeness to that flower. Their growth is compact compared with the large size of the showy, flat flowers, and this, combined with the fact that they are easy to grow and flower reliably, makes them the number one orchid for indoor culture. Their rise in popularity over recent years has been responsible for vast numbers of gorgeous hybrids being made available to the home grower.

These plants come in a wide range of colours, from dazzling white, through delicate pastel pinks and yellows, to the deepest of reds. The flowers are always adorned with a "mask" – a butterfly-shaped design at the centre of the bloom, on the base of the lip. The design takes many forms; it can be small and neat, or expand across the lip to form the "waterfall" patterns of great beauty and contrast. Two flower spikes are regularly produced from one pseudobulb, with from three to six 7cm (3in) wide blooms on each. Often blooming twice a year, in early summer and autumn, and accompanied by a delicate fragrance, it is easy to see why these orchids are so popular.

In a natural genus with thousands of hybrids, there are surprisingly few species. Of the five, all endemic to Colombia, four have contributed to the vast breeding programme that has enhanced the colour range tenfold. The evergreen, epiphytic species are all rare in cultivation and belong in specialized collections where they can be treasured for future generations.

Miltoniopsis are closely related to odontoglossums, with which they will readily interbreed, along with other members of this great alliance. When combined with odontoglossums, the resulting flowers have enlarged lips and strong colours. Miltoniopsis were originally placed in the genus *Miltonia*, which is now confined to about ten species found in Brazil, so when crossed with *Odontoglossum* they make *Odontonia*. Other intergeneric combinations that include *Miltoniopsis* (still called *Miltonia* for registration purposes) are *Miltassia* (*Miltonia* × *Brassia*), *Miltonidum* (*Miltonia* × *Oncidium*) and many others.

Hybrid miltoniopsis produce light green pseudobulbs that carry two apical and two basal, light green, narrowly oval leaves. The plants grow throughout most of the year, starting new growths as soon as the previous pseudobulb has been completed, and often before the plant has finished flowering. The flower spikes come quickly as the pseudobulb matures, and produce their blooms in an arching habit just clear of the foliage. The plants are seldom higher than 30cm (12in), which makes them ideal for the home grower.

Like all orchids, miltoniopsis thrive when surrounded by the foliage of other plants, and growing them in company means that the humidity can be maintained around them.

Miltoniopsis **Herr Alexandre**

Miltoniopsis **Jersey**

Temperature: Cool-growing.
Cultivation: Grow in pots of fine bark compost (growing medium) or in Rockwool. Keep them out of direct sunlight at all times. Water throughout the year and feed from spring to autumn.
Height: To 30cm (12in).

Miltoniopsis **Herr Alexandre**

This boldly marked, enchanting, white hybrid has all the hallmarks of a winning combination. The large flowers, 10cm (4in) wide, stand well clear of the foliage, appearing in early summer and autumn. Two flower spikes may be produced by the leading pseudobulb.

Miltoniopsis **Jersey**

A lovely red and white modern hybrid for summer flowering, this clone will produce up to six large blooms, 8cm (3in) wide, known affectionately as pansy orchids.

Miltoniopsis **Marie Riopelle 'Portland Rose'**

This wonderfully decorative hybrid has the exquisite lip marking, which combines with the deep, rosy pink of the rest of the flower to create a ravishing effect. Plants like this can be grown indoors or in a cool greenhouse where it is shady and moist. It flowers in late spring and early summer.

Miltoniopsis **Marie Riopelle 'Portland Rose'**

Miltoniopsis **Red Knight 'Grail' AM/RHS**
Producing a single, large flower in late spring and early summer, this hybrid has the appearance of deep red velvet. Young plants often produce one flower, but there can be up to six on an older plant.

Miltoniopsis **Rozel**
Many hybrids such as this have been bred to show the "waterfall" or "water droplet" patterning on the lip, which is a feature of these varieties. Note the occasional "droplet" on the petals. The combination of dark pink sepals and the beautifully patterned lips with their pink edge in this hybrid is captivating. The flowers appear in late spring and early summer.

Miltoniopsis **Saint Helier 'Pink Delight'**
A superb shape and rich pink colouring combine to make this lovely hybrid an absolute beauty. The deep crimson, butterfly-shaped mask at the centre of the blooms sets the scene for the paler heavy veining on the lip. Flowering occurs twice a year, in late spring and early summer.

Miltoniopsis **Rozel**

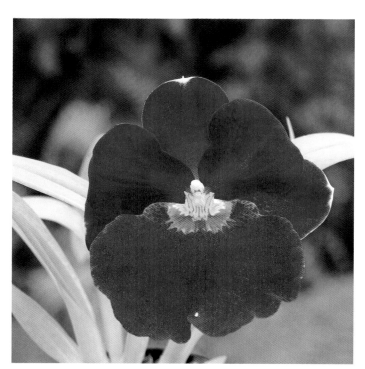

Miltoniopsis **Red Knight 'Grail' AM/RHS**

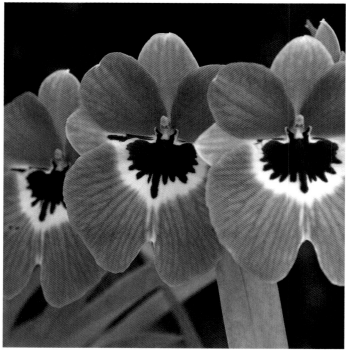

Miltoniopsis **Saint Helier 'Pink Delight'**

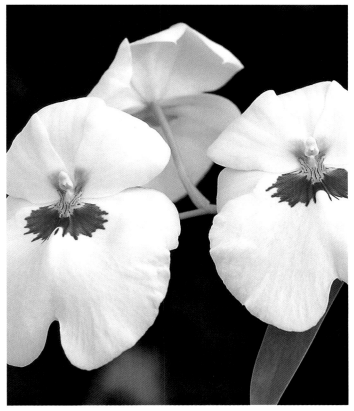

Miltoniopsis vexillaria

Miltoniopsis vexillaria 'Arctic Moon'

Miltoniopsis vexillaria

This soft pink form of the species, which comes from Colombia, is now a rare collectors' item. It is behind the majority of today's fine hybrids, which retain its lovely shape and gently arching habit. It flowers in late spring and early summer.

Miltoniopsis vexillaria 'Arctic Moon'

A pale form of the species, this lacks the delicate pink colouring of the sepals, petals and lip, but has an enhanced colour at the centre of the flower. It flowers in late spring and early summer.

Miltoniopsis Zorro 'Yellow Delight'

Selected breeding has produced this yellow hybrid, which flowers in late spring and early summer, although the colour does not exist in the species. It has been brought out from *Miltoniopsis roezlii*, the influence of which is also seen in the red marking.

Miltoniopsis Zorro 'Yellow Delight'

ODONTOGLOSSUM ALLIANCE

Odontoglossums are at the pinnacle of this complex alliance, which is made up of a number of closely related natural genera, all of which will interbreed to produce the fantastic range of flower types.

The species number about 60 evergreen epiphytic plants, which originate from high in the Andes of South America. Adored from the beginning of their introduction, the pristine white flowers of the splendid *Odontoglossum crispum* earned them the name "Queen of Orchids". They were so highly prized that demand led to their near extinction in the wild. Many superb varieties were grown that exist today only in the illustrations and descriptions of old publications. The comparatively few species grown today are confined to specialist collections, while in their place have come hundreds of hybrids that, for the hobby grower, constitute a much better buy. The hybrids have a spectrum of colours and a vigorous habit that are not found in the species, and are much more suited to mass-production for the hobbiest.

Typically, odontoglossums and related genera produce green pseudobulbs with an apical pair of mid-green, narrowly oval leaves, and two shorter leaves at the base. The plants may be 30–45cm (12–18in) high, and the flower spikes can be twice this. The flowers of the pure *Odontoglossum* hybrids are well rounded, with sepals and petals of equal size, and a neat, often frilly-edged lip. All colours are possible, with intricate patternings not found to the same extent in any other orchid. The flowers, which may number up to a dozen and are 6cm (2½in) wide, may be boldly marked or self-coloured. They will last for many weeks at almost any time of the year.

More numerous than the pure odontoglossums are the intergeneric hybrids. These include *Odontioda*, which is *Odontoglossum* crossed with the smaller, lesser-grown genus *Cochlioda*. This latter genus found fame for its bright red colouring, which it imparted to the *Odontioda* hybrids and which distinguishes them from odontoglossums. When combined with *Oncidium*, which is a genus dominated by smaller-flowered, longer-spiked, generally yellow flowers, the resulting *Odontocidium* produces some very pleasing results. There are many more combinations, all containing the genes of odontoglossums and exhibiting various characteristics belonging to the other partners. Some lines of breeding have concentrated on producing plants for the cooler climate, and include *Vuylstekeara* (*Cochlioda* × *Miltonia* × *Odontoglossum*) and *Wilsonara* (*Cochlioda* × *Odontoglossum* × *Oncidium*). By introducing the warmer-growing oncidiums to the equation, multigeneric hybrids have been raised that are heat-tolerant and can be grown in the tropics. These include *Beallara* (*Brassia* × *Cochlioda* × *Miltonia* × *Odontoglossum*) and *Aliceara* (*Brassia* × *Miltonia* × *Oncidium*).

Miltonidum **Pupukea Sunset**

Odontioda Avranches

Odontioda La Couperon

Odontoglossums can suffer easily from heat stress, and if you cannot keep the plants cool enough in summer, try putting them out of doors in a well-shaded place where they can be kept moist and humid. If placed in too much light, the leaves will turn a reddish hue. If not overdone, this is an acceptable colour that will return to green when the sun loses its power. However, if the exposure is excessive, the whole leaf surface will become dark red and premature leaf loss may result. Odontoglossums that lose too many leaves at one time will go into decline, and the plants will need to be repotted at the earliest opportunity, and the leafless pseudobulbs removed to restore the balance of the plant.

All the intergeneric odontoglossums are extremely lovely plants to grow, but care must be taken to ensure that the pseudobulbs stay plump throughout the year. On occasion, a mature plant will produce a tall, well-flowered spike that is more than it can support. As the buds develop to opening stage, the plant will suddenly shrivel badly, which is an indication that the flowers are sapping

its strength and it cannot support them and live. Remove the flower spike immediately. You can still enjoy the flowers by placing them in water. Repot the plant if necessary and encourage it to produce a new growth as quickly as possible, after which a slow recovery can begin.

Odontoglossums originally extended from the Andes in South America north to Mexico. Recent reclassification has created new genera, until the only true *Odontoglossum* species left occur in the Andes. Horticulturally, many of the older generic names are retained, hence both names, which remain in common usage, are given here. The exception is the genus *Rossioglossum*, where the species are so distinct that they are listed separately under Specialist Orchids.

Temperature: Cool-growing; keep below 24°C (75°F) in summer.
Cultivation: Grow in fine bark in 5–7cm (2–3in) pots that restrict the roots. Keep well shaded in summer, but give more light in winter. Water and apply feed all year, but give less in winter.
Height: 30–45cm (12–18in).

Miltonidum Pupukea Sunset

An unlikely cross between the tall-growing *Miltonia warscewiczii* and the diminutive *Oncidium cheirophorum* has resulted in this extremely attractive primary with flower spikes that reach 23cm (9in) in length. The flowers, with their cream, pink and green colouring appear in spring.

Odontioda Avranches

The artificial genus *Odontioda* (*Odontoglossum* × *Cochlioda*) was first produced to give the red colouring of the *Cochlioda* genus to the usually pale-coloured odontoglossums. In this largely spring-flowering hybrid, all *Cochlioda* influence has disappeared to return to the white colouring of the *Odontoglossum*.

Odontioda La Couperon

The vivid pink colouring and fine, deep pink patterning of the flowers on the long, arching flower spike reveal the influence of *Cochlioda* on this striking hybrid, which has given the flower its bright, vibrant appearance. The flowers appear at various times, but usually in the spring.

Odontioda Mont Felard × St Aubin's Bay

Odontioda Les Plantons

The colouring and patterning seen in this largely spring-flowering hybrid is typical of the diversity that is being bred into this man-made genus. The spots and blotches appear in a kaleidoscope of changing colours unequalled by any other orchid.

Odontioda Mont Felard × St Aubin's Bay

This is a neat-growing orchid, which, in varying seasons, produces spikes of white flowers spotted with rich pink; the lips are stained the same colour towards the edge and have yellow centres. The petal edges are ruffled and frilled.

Odontioda Pontinfer

With its beautifully proportioned flower in stunning red on white, this large, often branching flower spike shows the influence of the species *Odontoglossum pescatorei* in its background. The flowers appear at various times.

Odontioda Les Plantons

Odontioda Pontinfer

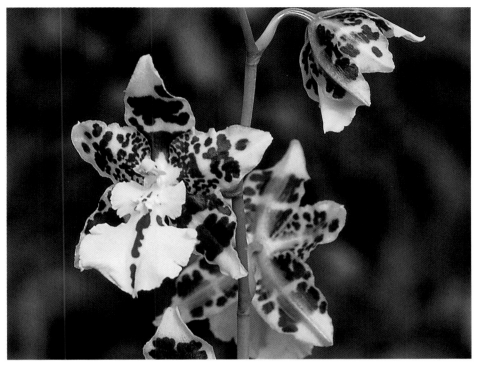

Odontocidium Isler's Gold Dragon

Bright colour combinations and a tall flower spike make this plant an indoor favourite. Grow in a cool situation where there is good light all year. The flowers, which appear at various times, will last for several weeks.

Odontocidium La Moye

This complex hybrid is robust and free-flowering. Keep the plant in a cool room in good light. Water and apply feed all year. The white flowers, with their pink and yellow patterning, will last for several weeks and appear at various times.

Odontocidium Russikon's Goldbaum

This bigeneric hybrid has inherited the large yellow lip and brown marking on the petals from the species *Oncidium tigrinum*. This has also contributed to the upright, branching habit of the spike. The flowers appear at various times, usually in spring.

Odontocidium Russikon's Goldbaum

Odontocidium Isler's Gold Dragon

Odontocidium La Moye

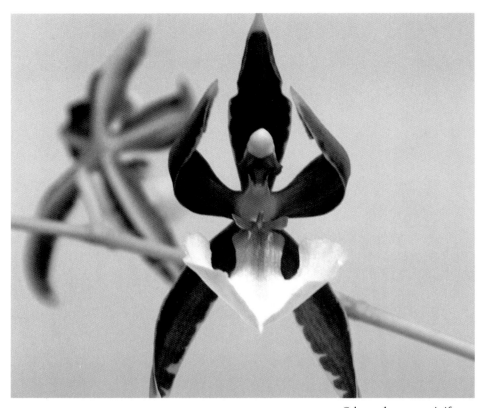

Odontoglossum cariniferum

Odontoglossum cariniferum
(syn. *Oncidium cariniferum*)

This lovely species celebrates its abundant spring flowering with a tall, branching spike which is heavy with blooms. Individually, these are rich chocolate brown, and the petals curve inwards to welcome the bloom's pollinator.

Odontoglossum cordatum
(syn. *Lemboglossum cordatum*)

This compact species carries its elegantly pointed, brown-blotched flowers in spring on a neat spike, about 15cm (6in) tall. Originating from Honduras, it is easy to grow and flower, and will do well indoors or in a cool, shady greenhouse.

Odontoglossum crocidipterum

Many *Odontoglossum* species are very rare today, as is this delicately patterned variety. The light yellow and brown markings are typical of a number in the genus that are mostly high-altitude plants from the Andes. This species flowers in spring.

Odontoglossum cordatum

Odontoglossum crocidipterum

Odontoglossum hallii

Odontoglossum hallii

With its strangely twisting, fragrant flowers and needle-like point to the lips, this summer-flowering species from Ecuador has contributed its basic yellow colouring to many early hybrids. It is quite rare in cultivation today.

Odontoglossum Jorisianum

This classic hybrid was first raised around the beginning of the 20th century, when hybridizing was not far advanced. It is the result of crossing two excellent species, *Odontoglossum purpureum* and *O. triumphans*, both of which are rare today. The red-marked, yellow flowers bloom in spring.

Odontoglossum laeve
(syn. *Miltonioides laevis*)

Strongly perfumed, this species carries its yellow and brown flowers with lips that are pink at the centre and held on a 45cm (18in) spike, well clear of the foliage. Flowering is in late summer and is long lasting. The plant is a robust grower, and comes from Honduras and Mexico.

Odontoglossum laeve

Odontoglossum Jorisianum

Odontoglossum oerstedii
(syn. *Ticoglossum oerstedii*)
An unusual and rarely seen species, this orchid has small pseudobulbs and leaves about 15cm (6in) tall. The pretty, waxy, white flowers with a golden yellow blotch on the lips appear on short spikes just above the foliage. Flowering in spring, this Costa Rican species can be grown warmer than most in the genus.

Vuylstekeara **Cambria 'Lensings Favorit'**
From the multitude of mass-produced Cambria 'Plush' came this "sport", showing sufficient variation of colouring to warrant its own specific varietal name. A lovely distinct form, with pink-blotched, red sepals and petals and a pink lip with a red central marking, it is suitable for indoors or a cool to intermediate greenhouse. The flowers bloom at various times of year.

Vuylstekeara **Cambria 'Plush' FCC/RHS**
One of the most popular orchids of all time, this multi-generic hybrid, with red and white colouring, has been produced in its thousands for the world pot-plant market. The large flowers, 7cm (3in) wide, are richly coloured and produced at various times throughout the year.

Odontoglossum oerstedii

Vuylstekeara Cambria 'Lensings Favorit'

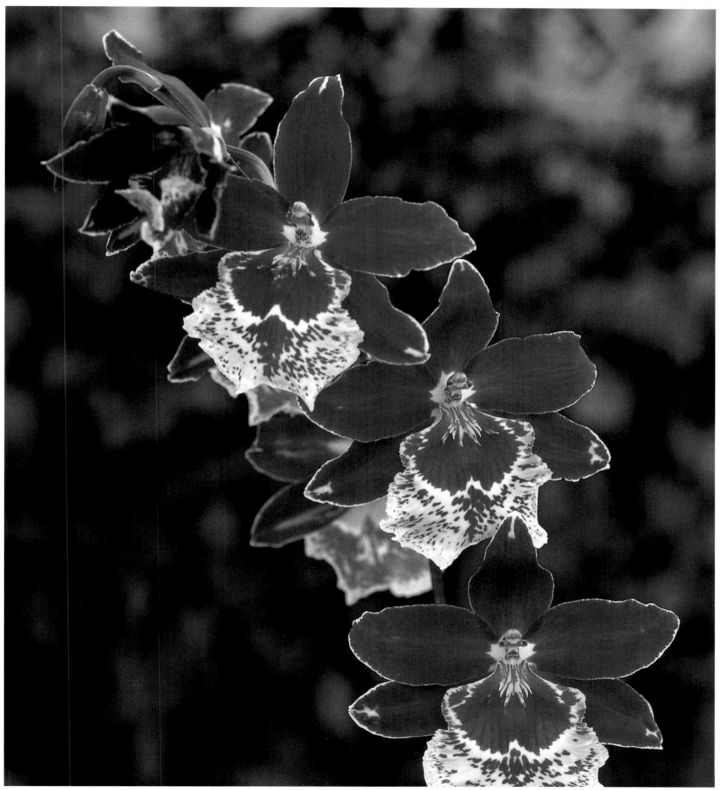

Vuylstekeara Cambria 'Plush' FCC/RHS

ONCIDIUM ALLIANCE

Among the 400 or so *Oncidium* species are many extremely varied plants, which range from diminutive equitants – small, fan-like, foliaged plants with brightly coloured flowers – to large-bulbed, long-spiked beauties such as *Oncidium macranthum*, now also known as *Cyrtochilum macranthum*. In between, are numerous, delightful plants of modest size with brightly coloured blooms which are predominantly yellow. Many of the species are in cultivation, and these are easy to grow and flower, finding favour among beginners for their reliability. To this pretty and interesting selection can be added a huge array of hybrids, mostly intergenerics resulting from crossings with odontoglossums and other related genera. The result is that many exciting and desirable plants are regularly seen that will grace any small orchid collection to perfection.

Oncidiums are evergreen plants, typically with neat, green pseudobulbs and a pair of narrowly oval leaves. The flower spikes come from the base of the leading pseudobulb as it matures, and this can be at almost any time of the year, although flowering peaks during the autumn months. The species originate from throughout tropical America and are found in varying epiphytic habitats. A number of species are know affectionately as "mule ear" types, a reference to their thick, solitary leaves that are supported by an often diminutive pseudobulb. These plants, which include *Oncidium luridum*, exist in hot, dry environments that are different to the Brazilian home of *O. flexuosum*, which resembles the typical *Odontoglossum*. The latter produces its pseudobulbs well spaced along an upward-growing rhizome. Grown on a piece of cork bark and given its freedom, this species produces a mass of white aerial roots, forming a curtain of a yard or so long.

In cultivation, some oncidiums are more favoured than others. The most popular kinds are cool-growing and do well when grown with odontoglossums, where they will co-exist under the same conditions. The mule ear types and others that come from the more tropical parts of America need to be kept warmer, and intermediate to warm conditions suit them best. They are high-light plants, requiring more light then their cooler-growing relations. In the northern hemisphere, some of them, such as *Oncidium splendidum*, can be challenging to flower because of the lack of year-round sunshine.

If you have limited growing space, look out for a few of the smaller-growing species or hybrids. These include *Oncidium cheirophorum*, which has short flower spikes of densely clustered, curiously shaped, bright yellow flowers.

Oncidium **Boissiense**

Similar in size is the highly fragrant *O. ornithorhynchum*, with its pretty pink blooms produced in profusion; this is a must. *O. flexuosum*, mentioned earlier, produces long flower spikes which terminate in a shower of numerous, bright yellow blooms which last for three or four weeks during the autumn.
Temperature: Cool-growing; some intermediate- to warm-growing.
Cultivation: Grow in 5–10cm (2–4in) pots of bark-based compost (growing medium). *O. flexuosum* can also be grown on bark. Shade cool-growing types in summer, but keep mule-ear types well-lit at all times. Water and feed hybrids throughout the year; keep species dry during winter, when growth stops.
Height: 15–30cm (6–12in).

Oncidium Boissiense
This striking hybrid bears large, bright yellow flowers with the huge lip being derived from the species *Oncidium varicosum*, among others. This strong, robust, autumn-flowering plant can be grown indoors or in a cool to intermediate greenhouse.

Oncidium obryzatum
The tall, wispy flower spikes of this yellow-flowered species provide a dense swarm of tiny blooms that hover above the 20cm (8in) plant in winter. This species should be grown in an intermediate greenhouse.

Oncidium Sharry Baby 'Sweet Fragrance'
This lovely, chocolate-scented hybrid produces a profusion of cherry-red blooms with white-tipped lips. It blooms at various times and is cool-growing. The flowers show a strong influence from the species *Oncidium ornithorhynchum*, which appears in its background.

Oncidium sphacelatum

This is one of the taller-growing *Oncidium* species. The branching flower spikes can reach 1m (3ft) tall, with numerous flowers on side branches. This native of Mexico needs good light in order to bloom well in the spring.

Oncidium **Sharry Baby 'Sweet Fragrance'**

Oncidium obryzatum

Oncidium sphacelatum

PAPHIOPEDILUM

Aeons ago, the paphiopedilums, and other related slipper orchids, split from the mainstream to evolve along their own path. This led to the characteristic pouch that defines this and related genera. The pouch, or slipper, is a modification of the third petal, which appears in other orchids as the lip. In developing the pouch, the typical *Paphiopedilum* modified its other parts accordingly. The two lateral sepals, for instance, have largely become fused and are mostly hidden from view behind the pouch. The pouch is designed to trap a pollinating insect by first enticing it to the edge, where it then loses its grip on the slippery surface and tumbles in. Once inside the pouch, a ladder of small hairs enables the insect to force its way out between either side of the pouch and the column. As it does so, the insect takes the pollen with it.

The paphiopedilums include about 65 species found throughout the Far East, from India, China and South-east Asia to the Philippines, Indonesia and New Guinea. They are evergreen plants without pseudobulbs, mostly terrestrial, producing tufted growths, from the centre of which extends the flower spike. The spikes may have a solitary flower, or carry from two to a dozen blooms. Some of the most striking of all orchid blooms are those produced by the Borneo species, *Paphiopedilum rothschildianum*, where the lateral petals have become extremely long and narrow, held horizontally and dramatically striped. When seen on a tall flower spike, the result is nothing short of heart-stopping.

New introductions from China, brought into cultivation during the last two decades of the 20th century, have revolutionized new breeding lines. Species such as the golden yellow *Paphiopedilum armeniacum* and the delightful, pink *P. micranthum*, among others, have resulted in some superb hybrids with unique colour combinations.

Paphiopedilums are noted for their longevity. Among the first of the orchids to be hybridized in the 19th century, there are plants in collections today that are over 150 years old. These grand plants have become classics in their own right and are treasured possessions in the collections of those fortunate enough to have acquired them.

So great is the appeal of the paphiopedilums that whole collections are devoted to this one genus. For the beginner or collector, there are several kinds to look out for. The complex hybrids produce plants with stout green foliage and a single, large, rounded bloom in a variety of colours, from yellow and green through to red, brown and bronze. The flowers may be self-coloured, or heavily spotted and shaded with other colours. All produce highly glossed blooms, mostly during the winter months when they will last for many weeks.

The mottled-leaved types produce plants of a smaller stature, and can be extremely free-flowering on a large, multi-growthed plant. The flower spikes are taller, up to 30cm (12in) tall, with a single, open-shaped bloom. These less heavy blooms can be green or red, with the darkest colours being deep purple bordering on the elusive black. These

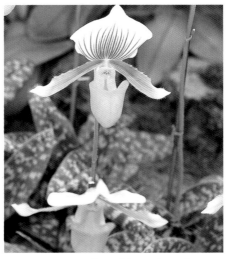

***Paphiopedilum* Claire de Lune**

handsome blooms are usually striped or spotted, often with dramatically flamed dorsal petals. Their flowering season extends into the summer, overlapping a further group that produces multi-flowering spikes. These are hybrids bred from species such as the extremely long-petalled *Paphiopedilum sanderianum* and *P. rothschildianum*, with its rigidly held petals. These, and *P. parishii*, with its long twisting petals, have produced some lovely hybrids that add a dramatic dimension to the genus.

Paphiopedilums produce sparse roots compared with other orchids; these are brown and hairy. Repotting is best done on an annual basis but with minor disturbance to the root system. They should be kept in as small a pot as possible, often being placed back into the same size pot after repotting and having the compost (growing medium) replaced with a fresh supply.

When in bloom, paphiopedilums will need some support. Use a thin split bamboo cane to hold the spike upright, and wait until the bloom is open and has become "set". At this stage, tie the cane at the base of the flower to bring it up to eye level, where it can be fully appreciated.

Temperature: Intermediate-growing.
Cultivation: Grow in bark-based compost (growing medium) or rock wool, in pots that restrict the roots. Place them away from direct sun and keep them evenly moist all year. Feed regularly. Mist only lightly (if at all) to avoid water running into the centre of the growths, where it can lead to rotting.
Height: 15–30cm (6–12in).

Paphiopedilum Claire de Lune

This is an older hybrid that has stood the test of time and is as popular today as it was over 100 years ago. The plants have beautifully mottled leaves and the elegant green-and-white flowers are carried on slender stems in winter and spring.

Paphiopedilum Corbiere 'La Tuilerie'

Paphiopedilum delenatii

Paphiopedilum haynaldianum

Paphiopedilum Corbiere 'La Tuilerie'

The elegant lines of this older-type, spring-flowering hybrid with its rich red colouring and deeply veined dorsal petal make an attractive combination. The stems are 23cm (9in) tall on a green-leaved plant.

Paphiopedilum delenatii

Originating from Vietnam, this enticing, pale pink species, with its slightly deeper pink lip, makes an attractive plant with mottled foliage. The flowers of this species, which bloom in the spring, have passed their delicate pink colouring on to many newer hybrids.

Paphiopedilum haynaldianum

One of the finest of the multi-flowered species, this large-flowered plant, which has flowers 13cm (5in) across, originates from India and carries its delectable flowers in green, brown and pink on a 60cm (2ft) flower spike in winter.

Paphiopedilum insigne

This was once a very popular species, grown by the million to provide cut flowers. Today, it makes a lovely houseplant, with its green and brown colouring. It grows well in a cool room out of the sun where it will bloom freely during the winter.

Paphiopedilum insigne

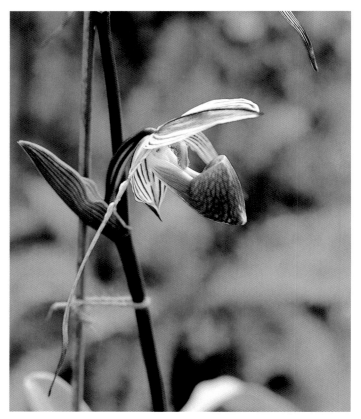

Paphiopedilum Leeanum

Paphiopedilum Lady Isabel

Paphiopedilum Jersey Freckles

This combination of chocolate brown, lime, cream and pale pink is very striking in this large-flowered hybrid. It grows in a fairly warm situation so long as the leaves are not exposed to direct sun. The flowers appear in winter.

Paphiopedilum Lady Isabel

This hybrid is an offspring of *Paphiopedilum rothschildianum*. The multi-flowered spike on a tall stem has cream flowers, streaked with brown and with a pale red lip, which appear in winter and spring. The long, green leaves can become quite large.

Paphiopedilum Leeanum

This fine old hybrid was raised in Victorian times. The flowers have green lateral sepals, a pink-speckled, white dorsal sepal and a brown pouch. They appear during winter and last up to three months on the plant.

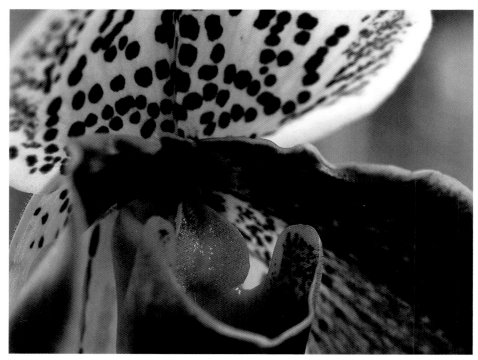

Paphiopedilum Jersey Freckles

Paphiopedilum **Les Landes**

Among the green-leaved hybrids, such as this large, red-brown variety, are a number with highly glossed flowers in all shades from dark red and bronze through green and yellow. The flowers, usually appearing singly on the stem in spring, can be as much as 10cm (4in) across.

Paphiopedilum micranthum

This species from China has neat, mottled leaves and huge-pouched, pale pink flowers with deep pink and yellow stripes on the petals. The flowers appear singly on medium-length stems in spring. The blooms have the bulbous pouch more usually associated with the cypripediums.

Paphiopedilum **Quetivel Mill**
× **Rod McLellan**

This is a tall-stemmed, green-leaved hybrid which is suitable for indoors or a shady intermediate greenhouse. These hybrids mainly bloom in winter, when the red-freckled, yellow flowers will last for many weeks. The dorsal sepal is edged with white.

Paphiopedilum **Les Landes**

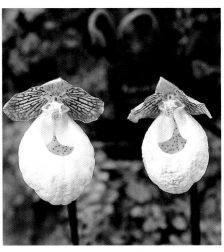

Paphiopedilum micranthum

Paphiopedilum **Schillerianum**

This old primary hybrid, which flowers in winter, could be over 200 years old, but may well be from a later remake of the same cross. The dominant parent here is the slender-petalled *P. rothschildianum*. The creamy green flowers are striped and spotted with deep purple, and the bulbous pouch is similarly coloured in purple.

Paphiopedilum **Yellow Tiger**

This lovely, multi-flowered cross between the similar, long-petalled species *Paphiopedilum stonei* and *P. granduliferum* was raised in California in 1984. The creamy white, winter flowers are striped with chocolate brown, while the pouch is raspberry coloured. The pale green petals complete the subtle effect.

Paphiopedilum **Quetivel Mill** × **Rod McLellan**

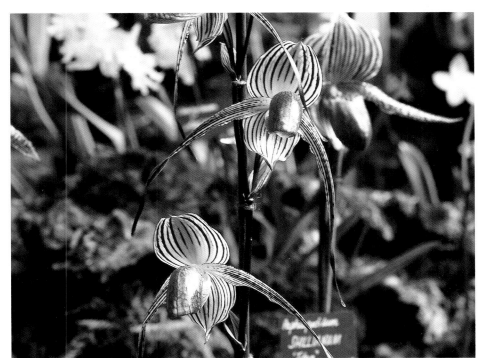

Paphiopedilum **Yellow Tiger**

Paphiopedilum **Schillerianum**

PHALAENOPSIS ALLIANCE

These orchids enjoy an extremely high profile among growers and beginners alike. The genus has probably done more in recent years to popularize orchids than any other. This has arisen from the mass-hybridizing that has taken place in parts of the world where these orchids can be raised with comparative ease and shipped to the wholesale market. Hybridizing continued at an amazing rate during the latter part of the 20th century, when more phalaenopsis were being produced for the mass-market than any other orchid, even beating cymbidiums in the popularity stakes. This has meant that phalaenopsis are sold in various outlets from florists to DIY stores, where they offer extremely good value for money.

Phalaenopsis are everybody's orchid – they can be grown with great ease indoors, where they require the minimum of care to produce numerous flowers over an extended period. They are ideally suited to the home environment, and their popularity was established when it was realised what excellent houseplants they make. Being warm, shade-loving plants, the interior of most houses is an ideal environment for them, often better than an overheated, over-bright greenhouse.

Phalaenopsis will also interbreed with other related genera such as *Ascocenda* and *Doritaenopsis*, and through *Rhynchostylis* to *Vanda*, resulting in some extremely complex and incredible, artificial genera.

The natural genus of *Phalaenopsis* is made up of almost 50 species, originating from the Old World through India, South-east Asia, Indonesia and parts of Australia. Most are evergreen epiphytic plants. The greatest concentration, and the species that

have had the greatest influence on hybridizing, come from the Philippine Islands. These include *Phalaenopsis amabilis*, *P. stuartiana*, *P. sanderiana* and *P. schilleriana*, which are long-stemmed varieties with pink or white flowers. The plants are mostly extremely attractive, their broad, fleshy leaves often marbled with light and dark green mottling. They are monopodial in their growth, each new leaf extending from a centre, with the flower spikes coming from the base of the lower leaves. Phalaenopsis do not grow overly large, because leaves are shed from the base at about the same rate as new ones are developed. Their roots are exceptionally good-looking, often appearing above the pot and remaining airborne. These are flattened and silvery white, with clearly visible, green-growing tips. They have a tendency to adhere to any surface with which they come into contact. In a greenhouse, they often attach themselves to the bench upon which they are growing. Roots that have meandered over the rim of the pot are impossible to get back without snapping. Allow them to wander at will, and, when repotting, leave any live aerial roots outside the pot. Any that have died and are shrivelled can be cut off.

In addition to the long-stemmed, large-flowered kinds, there are numerous other hybrids raised from smaller, yellow- or brown-coloured species, which have given rise to a further dimension within the alliance. Many delightful miniature varieties are now available, with a colour range that extends from white, through yellow, to pink and red. These include pure phalaenopsis and intergeneric hybrids. The choice has become immense.

Phalaenopsis can bloom at almost any time, and it is not unusual for one plant to bloom two or three times in one year and to remain in bloom for many months. It is important, however, that the plant continues to make new leaves at the same time as flowering. If too many leaves are shed, you should cut off any flowering spikes and allow the plant to grow on until it has three or four leaves before allowing it to produce flowers. With half a dozen plants in an indoor environment, you can achieve almost perpetual, year-round flowering.

Temperature: Warm-growing (winter minimum 18°C/65°F with a rise during the day of 12°C/20°F).

Cultivation: Grow in 10cm (4in) pots of coarse bark or Rockwool. Water and feed throughout the year, but avoid

Doritaenopsis **Kiska**

Phalaenopsis **Barbara Moler** × **Spitzberg**

Phalaenopsis **Brother Lancer**

Phalaenopsis **Claire de Valec**

Phalaenopsis **Catalina**

Phalaenopsis **Culiacan**

waterlogging. High humidity is not necessary; placing plants on a humidity tray provides the appropriate level. Wipe the foliage with a damp cloth to clear of dust, but do not allow water to run down into the centre of the plant, where it can lead to rotting.
Height: 15cm (6in).

Doritaenopsis **Kiska**
This bigeneric hybrid, which combines the genera *Phalaenopsis* with *Doritis*, is usually darker in colour. This pale variety shows a new colour breakthrough with the striking orange lip. The flowers bloom in all seasons.

Phalaenopsis **Barbara Moler × Spitzberg**
This is a new hybrid from this extremely popular genus which adapts so well to indoor culture. The plant likes to be kept warm and moist all year, but out of direct sun. The pale lemon flowers have an orange lip and can appear at any time.

Phalaenopsis **Brother Lancer**
This is a smaller-flowered hybrid that carries its pretty blooms on a shorter, more compact spike, making it ideal for growing indoors where space is limited. The flowers, which can appear at any time of year, are pale lemon, striped and speckled with pink, and have a deep orange lip.

Phalaenopsis **Catalina**
Many *Phalaenopsis* hybrids are pure white with lovely marking on the lip. This varies between similar hybrids; in this case, the lip is orange. The flowers bloom in all seasons.

Phalaenopsis **Claire de Valec**
This robust grower produces long sprays of pale pink flowers in all seasons. It has proved to be consistent as a show plant and is a parent of further fine crosses.

Phalaenopsis **Culiacan**
This lovely hybrid has white flowers with a golden yellow lip. A well-grown plant will bloom two or three times a year.

Phalaenopsis **Fajan's Fireworks**

Phalaenopsis **Flare Spots**

Phalaenopsis Fajan's Fireworks

Intricate pink veining overlies the white background on this lovely hybrid, which are affectionately known as candy stripes. The sprays of flowers, 7cm (3in) wide, can last for many weeks at various times of the year.

Phalaenopsis Flare Spots

This hybrid has a compact flower spike, with the blooms set close together on the 30cm (12in) tall stem. The blooms are just under 8cm (3in) across. The white flowers, which appear in all seasons, have purple speckling and a crimson lip.

Phalaenopsis Follett

This tall-stemmed, large-flowered, pink-striped hybrid, which flowers in all seasons, is typical of those being produced in vast quantities for the houseplant trade. These orchids are unbeatable for indoors.

Phalaenopsis Golden Hat

Slight red peppering at the centre of these light yellow flowers makes an interesting combination of colour. In this modern hybrid, numerous flowers are produced on a branching flower spike in all seasons.

Phalaenopsis Happy Girl

This white hybrid, with lovely rounded petals and a cherry-red lip, provides an ideal combination of colours. The flowers, on an arching flower spike, fall into a cascade and appear in all seasons.

Phalaenopsis **Follett**

Phalaenopsis **Golden Hat**

Phalaenopsis **Happy Girl**

Phalaenopsis Hawaiian Darling   *Phalaenopsis* Lady Sakhara   *Phalaenopsis* Little Skipper

Phalaenopsis Hawaiian Darling

This almost-white flower has fine red peppering at the centre of the bloom, and the lip is leopard-marked with red spotting. This is an ideal hybrid for growing indoors. The flower spikes can reach 45cm (18in) in height. The flowers appear in all seasons.

Phalaenopsis Lady Sakhara

Throughout the year, this striking epiphytic orchid produces racemes of pink flowers that are veined darker; the lips are glowing cerise pink and have yellow centres.

Phalaenopsis Little Skipper

Miniature hybrids are really taking off now, as this popular variety shows. In all seasons, the branching sprays produce numerous, pale pink, small flowers, each no more than 2.5cm (1in) across, to create a charming picture.

Phalaenopsis Little Skipper 'Zuma Nova'

Raised in the United States to give large sprays of small, pink flowers in all seasons, this variety offers a distinct contrast to the larger-flowered types. The plants are more compact and take up less room.

Phalaenopsis Little Skipper 'Zuma Nova'

Phalaenopsis **Mad Milva**

Phalaenopsis **Purple Valley**

Phalaenopsis Mad Milva

This plant will do well as the centrepiece of an orchid display, provided it is kept out of direct sunlight. The flowers are delightful, with cerise pink petals and sepals, and a darker pink lip. The flowers appear in all seasons and will last for several weeks.

Phalaenopsis Mystik Golden Leopard

This lovely yellow hybrid was produced from species such as *Phalaenopsis amboinensis* to give a compact flowering spike on a smaller plant. The orange-red lip provides a striking colour contrast against the yellow flower. Flowering can occur at any time of the year.

Phalaenopsis Purple Valley

The deep cherry-red blooms of this hybrid are a huge step forward in the production of exciting new phalaenopsis varieties. The plant blooms on a tall flower spike in all seasons, which will remain for months on end.

Phalaenopsis Rendezvous

This superb, deep pink hybrid has darker veining covering the sepals and petals while the lip is a vibrantly rich red. This plant will bloom two or three times during the year.

Phalaenopsis **Mystik Golden Leopard**

Phalaenopsis **Rendezvous**

Phalaenopsis **Yellow Treasure**

Phalaenopsis schilleriana

This is one of the species from the Philippines from which most of the modern hybrids have been raised. The pale pink flowers, which appear in all seasons, are daintier and lack the rounded shape of the hybrids. The foliage is attractively mottled.

Phalaenopsis **Silky Moon**

This white orchid with an orange-red lip has tall flower spikes, which make an impressive display in any room in all seasons. When not in flower, keep in a warm situation away from direct sunlight.

Phalaenopsis **Yellow Treasure**

The light yellow-green colour of this neat hybrid is coming close to the more unusual green that has evaded hybridists to date. The flowers appear at any time of year. This is a flower with a future.

Phalaenopsis schilleriana

Phalaenopsis **Silky Moon**

PHRAGMIPEDIUM

Phragmipediums, like paphiopedilums, are also known as slipper orchids. However, there is no slipper orchid alliance as appears within the other major orchid groups, because phragmipediums will not interbreed with similar-looking, related genera. This is surprising when we consider the similarity between the flowers, especially among the multi-flowered paphiopedilums. The plants resemble the paphiopedilums, with their large, tufted growths.

Phragmipediums are mainly terrestrial or lithophytic plants, originating from South America, where they number possibly less than 20 species. The genus remained in the background of orchid cultivation until the last quarter of the 20th century, when a sensational new discovery revolutionized this previously drab-coloured genus. This new introduction was the famed *Phragmipedium besseae*, a plant with a flower of such brilliant red that it caused a sensation wherever it was seen. Its natural home was on the sheer rock faces of the inaccessible mountainous regions of Peru and Ecuador, and it was this precarious and impossible-to-reach habitat that kept the species under nature's wraps for so long. Invisible from the ground, it was only discovered when spotted from a helicopter flying over the area on a plant-hunting expedition. By the end of the 20th century, most of its former sites had been systematically stripped of these precious plants, which were quickly spread around the world. Today, this one plant has projected the genus to a high profile not previously enjoyed. Numerous red hybrids have resulted that are now at the forefront of all *Phragmipedium* breeding. We have yet to see the full potential this species is capable of reaching.

The majority of hybrids raised using the red-flowered *Phragmipedium besseae* have predictably produced blooms in the red to orange range. These are large-pouched, short-petalled, nicely balanced flowers, and are in sharp contrast to the species *Phragmipedium caudatum* and its old hybrid *P.* Grande, which possess extremely long, ribbon-like, twisting petals that reach down for 30cm (12in) or more. When held horizontally by the petal tips, the flower stretches over 60cm (2ft), making this the largest orchid flower in the world.

Phragmipediums become considerably large in their growth, and some of the modern hybrids raised from the species *Phragmipedium longifolium* produce extremely long, almost perpetually blooming flower spikes that go on for many months, even years, producing more blooms from an ever-extending tip. These large plants need plenty of headroom wherever they are grown. Their root system is similar to paphiopedilums, but more robust. The plants are at their best when allowed to reach their full potential and flowering

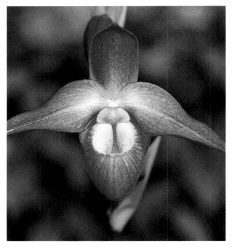

Phragmipedium **Dom Wimber**

ability, rather then being divided into small pieces. Give them the room they require and they will reward you with plenty of flowers.
Temperature: Intermediate-growing.
Cultivation: Grow in 15–20cm (6–8in) pots of coarse bark chips or Rockwool. Water freely throughout the year to keep the roots evenly moist. Feed at every other watering. Provide shade in summer, and give more light in winter.
Height: 30–60cm (1–2ft).

Phragmipedium besseae
This is the only known red-flowered *Phragmipedium* species, and one that was discovered as late as 1981 in Peru. This species, which flowers in summer, has revolutionized the genus by adding its red colouring to a new generation of hybrids.

Phragmipedium **Don Wimber**
This is an example of the lovely results that are being obtained by breeding with the species *Phragmipedium besseae*. The other parent is the hybrid *P.* Eric Young. The orange flowers are tinged with yellow, and appear in winter and spring on spikes up to 1m (3ft) high.

Phragmipedium besseae

Phragmipedium Grande

Phragmipedium Eric Young

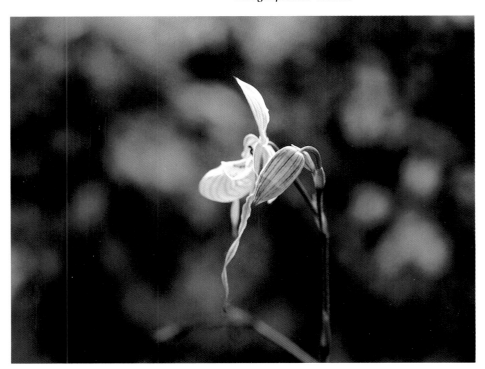

Phragmipedium pearcei

Phragmipedium Eric Young

This superb, winter- and spring-flowering modern hybrid was produced from the species *Phragmipedium besseae* to give the red colouring. The other parent of this primary hybrid is the long-petalled species *Phragmipedium longifolium*.

Phragmipedium Grande

This old hybrid produces large, green, long-petalled flowers in winter and spring, which droop from the multi-flowered spike. Although a great favourite, it lacks the colour of the modern hybrids.

Phragmipedium pearcei

This dwarf species from Central America has tufted growths and flower spikes 15cm (6in) high. The 10cm (4in) long, pale green flowers appear in spring and summer and have typically ribbon-like petals. Several flowers can appear on a stem.

PLEIONE

Pleiones are charming, miniature orchids with about 16 species in the genus. These are mainly terrestrial, sometimes lithophytic or epiphytic, deciduous plants, which produce rounded or coned pseudobulbs with a single, narrowly oval, ribbed leaf. The flowers are borne singly, but with occasionally two, on a slender stem that arises from the new growth when it is very young. The flowers are large for the size of the plant, and vary little in their appearance. Typically, the flowers have narrow sepals and petals of equal length, with a large, frilled, trumpet-shaped lip. The colours extend from pristine white to glistening pink and delicate mauve shades. Yellow is a rarer colour, but comes through in a number of the hybrids derived from the yellow-flowered species *Pleione forrestii*. While this species is rare in cultivation, others are common and easily grown alongside the larger, more richly coloured hybrids, which can have flowers 7cm (3in) across. Their flowering period is in the spring, although there are a few autumn-blooming species, such as *Pleione humilus*. The flowers will last for about ten days, after which new roots appear and the growth continues to complete the pseudobulb throughout the summer. As autumn approaches, the leaves will turn yellow before being discarded by the plant.

The pseudobulbs are only of two years' duration, so each spring pot up last season's pseudobulbs and remove the previous ones, which will be shrivelled and dead.

Pleiones like to be grown very cool, and a frost-free position will suit them during the winter. In summer, while they are growing, keep them on a cool windowsill or outdoors, if a suitable place can be found for them, once the flowers have finished. They can be planted out in rockeries in sheltered places, but the biggest danger here is of their being eaten by mice or slugs. Whatever other orchids you grow, find a small place for a few dainty pleiones.

Pleione formosana **var.** *alba*

Temperature: Very cool-growing.
Cultivation: Grow in groups in shallow pans or half pots of terrestrial orchid compost (growing medium), or a fine mixture of peat (or peat substitute) and perlite to which a little charcoal has been added. Give some shade in summer and full light in winter. Water only when in growth, from spring to autumn and feed at every other watering. Overwinter in a cool, dry place.
Height: To 15cm (6in).

Pleione formosana **var.** *alba*

This is the white form of the variable species that has done much for hybridizing within this genus. These deciduous orchids need a very cool winter's rest. The flowers appear in early spring.

Pleione speciosa

This very pretty species from China blooms in early spring from the centre of the new growth. The mauve flowers, with yellow at the centre of the lip, are 5cm (2in) across and appear on a stem less than 15cm (6in) tall. Many hybrids have been produced from this species.

Pleione speciosa

STANHOPEA

These are among the strangest of orchids, with their unusual habit of producing downward flower spikes that carry large, unwieldy flowers with fantastic fragrances and amazing shapes. To some, their appeal is irresistible, and they are worthy of interest.

About 25 species exist, originating from Central and South America where they grow as epiphytes on stout tree branches. The plants are evergreen, producing stout pseudobulbs with a single, large, semi-rigid leaf. They are grown in open hanging baskets to allow their flower spikes to penetrate the base and emerge through the bottom during the summer-flowering season. Under good culture they make extensive aerial roots, which form a dense and protective mass around the base of the plant. A good number of the species are in cultivation, in addition to a few hybrids, which are generally little improvement upon the fantastic species. Although the flowers are extremely short-lived, lasting for just a few days, plants that are grown to specimen size will produce several flower spikes, which open in succession to extend the flowering season.

Stanhopea **Boileau**

These orchids have a definite resting period during which they need to be allowed to dry out. This period may be while they are flowering in the summer, with new growths appearing during the autumn and continuing throughout the winter.
Temperature: Cool- to intermediate-growing.
Cultivation: Grow in open hanging baskets in bark-based compost (growing medium) in good light throughout the year. Water while in active growth and feed during the same period. Mist during summer, except when in flower.
Height: 30cm (12in).

Stanhopea **Boileau**
This is one of the very few hybrids in the genus. The blooms are short-lived, lasting just three to four days, but several flowerings can be expected in summer.

Stanhopea graveolans
Grow stanhopeas where you can provide them with plenty of headroom and space to accommodate their hanging flowers. This strongly fragrant species, from Mexico and Guatemala, blooms several times throughout the summer.

Stanhopea wardii
Stanhopeas are grown in open slatted baskets and their extraordinary flowers are produced on vertical flower spikes that hang below the plant. This highly fragrant species needs a cool greenhouse where it will flower throughout the summer. The yellow flowers have orange markings.

Stanhopea graveolens

Stanhopea wardii

VANDA ALLIANCE

Vandas are a natural genus of over 30 species, originating from a wide area of the Old World, from India, South-east Asia and Indonesia to the Philippines, New Guinea and Australia. They head a huge alliance of intergeneric hybrid forms, which include other natural genera such as *Ascocentrum*, *Rhynchostylis*, *Renanthera*, *Arachnis*, and many others, including *Phalaenopsis* and *Doritis*. The majority of these plants are warm-growing, light-loving types that grow best in the tropics, where a massive breeding programme has continued apace. The results can be seen in florists' shops where the cut flowers are in great demand.

Vandas are monopodial evergreen plants that grow from a central tip on an ever-extending rhizome. As new, semi-rigid leaves are produced from the apex, the lower ones are eventually lost. After a few years, the plants become "leggy" with a length of bare stem above the pot. Stout aerial roots, formed along the base stem, are a feature of these plants. At the right stage, the plant can be reduced in length by cutting through the bare rhizome below the aerial roots. The top portion is potted up, leaving the aerial roots outside the pot. In time, new roots will be made inside the pot and the plant will continue its upward progression. The flower spikes emerge from the axils of the lower leaves at various times throughout the year.

Some varieties are more easily flowered than others. Try a few of the fantastic blue or mauve hybrids, containing the species *Vanda coerulea* and *V.* (syn. *Eulanthe*) *sanderiana*. The crossing of these two plants produced the lovely, deep blue *V.* Rothschildiana, and this one hybrid has done more to promote the genus in the northern hemisphere than any other orchid. *V.* Rothschildiana will grow with exceptional ease and bloom two to three times a year. The plants can grow considerably tall, up to 1m (3ft), making an impressive specimen when in bloom. The large, rounded blooms are over 7cm (3in) across and will last for several weeks at a time. In addition, there are other variously coloured vandas and intergeneric hybrids available. Look out for the brilliantly coloured, often smaller-flowered ascocendas (*Vanda × Ascocentrum*). These are often more popular than the pure vandas because of their neat habit and upright flower spikes, which are crowded with beautiful, symmetrical flowers in fiery reds, gorgeous oranges and deep yellows. While some are self-coloured, others display extreme tessellating or mottling on the petals and sepals.

Temperature: Warm-growing.

Cultivation: Grow in open slatted baskets in a compost (growing medium) of coarse bark chips to which a few pieces of horticultural charcoal or pumice have been added. Maintain good light all year. Water freely and feed weekly in summer to encourage aerial roots. Mist the foliage on a regular basis.

Height: 30–100cm (12-36in).

Ascocenda **Crownfox Mystique**

Ascocenda Crownfox Gem

Trudelia cristata

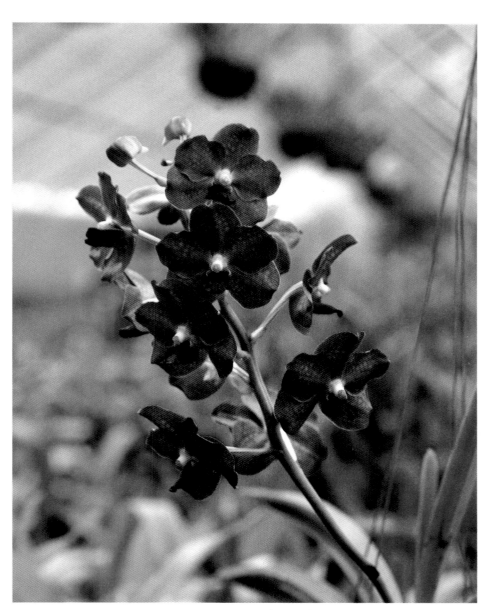

Ascocenda David Peterson × *Rhynchostylis coelestis*

Ascocenda Crownfox Gem

The rich russet-brown of this summer-flowering orchid is an unusual colour combination. The colour is the result of several lines of breeding using the colourful *Ascocentrum* species with *Vanda* hybrids.

Ascocenda Crownfox Mystique

The wonderfully rich colouring of this bigeneric cross has come from the *Ascocentrum* parent, which has also reduced the size of the summer flowers.

Ascocenda David Peterson × Rhynchostylis coelestis

This is a tri-generic genus in the huge *Vanda* alliance, which has produced vanda-like flowers, well rounded and tessellated, on an upright flower spike. The *Rhynchostylis* parent has reduced the overall size of the flowers, which otherwise closely resemble the pure *Vanda*. The striking, purple-blue flowers appear in abundant clusters in the summer.

Trudelia cristata

Closely allied to *Vanda*, where it was originally placed, this green-flowered species with a vivid, red-striped lip makes a slender plant that can grow to 30cm (12in) tall. This popular species, which flowers in the spring, comes from India.

Vanda coerulescens

Vanda Fuchs Magic

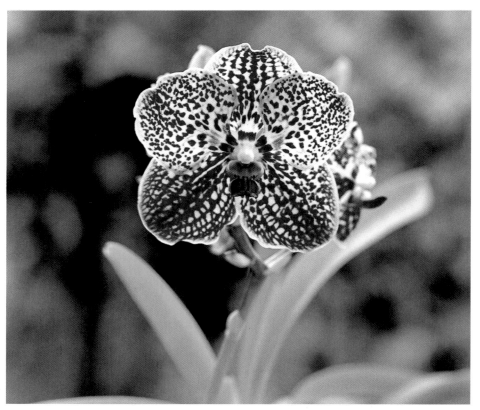

Vanda Gordon Dillon 'Lea' AM/AOS

Vanda coerulescens
One of the smaller-growing species, this plant has terete leaves in pairs with the loosely flowered spike coming from the leaf axils. The pale mauve flowers a violet lip are 3cm (1¼in) across. This highly variable species can bloom at various times.

Vanda Fuchs Magic
Among the numerous hybrids in this genus is a multitude of colourful varieties where the rich mauves and purples excel. This stunning variety, which flowers in summer, shows delicate tessellating over the sepals and petals.

Vanda Gordon Dillon 'Lea' AM/AOS
Awarded by the American Orchid Society for its unusual colour combination and flower quality, this striking hybrid speaks for itself. The flower spike is compact, and the heavy, textured blooms are evenly marked. The flowers appear in the summer.

Vanda Julia Sorenson

Vanda plants such as this hybrid can grow considerably large with many pairs of leaves. The large, 10cm (4in) flowers, which appear in summer, are produced on spikes that come from the axils of the leaves.

Vanda Manuvadee 'Sky'

Blue is a colour seldom met in orchids other than vandas. The deep purple-blue of this outstanding hybrid has come from several blue-flowered species, including *Vanda coerulea*. The flowers bloom in summer.

Vanda Julia Sorenson

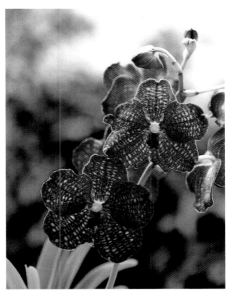

Vanda Manuvadee 'Sky'

ZYGOPETALUM

Strong colourings, fragrance and upright flower spikes typify this South and Central American genus. The plants are mainly epiphytic with stout pseudobulbs and leaves which can grow to 30cm (12in) or more in height. They produce a thick rooting system, not unlike that of cymbidiums. For this reason they need to be repotted on a regular basis, as if left too long in one pot they push themselves out by their roots. The flower spikes appear from the base of the new growth while it is still at a young stage in the spring. The flowers are characterized by their bold colourings, the petals and sepals (of equal length) being mostly green-brown or green speckled brown, and the bold lip usually white, veined, dotted or dashed with mauve or indigo blue. Of the 20 or so species that occur in the wild, only a few are generally found in cultivation, the most popular being *Zygopetalum mackaii*.

Until recently very little hybridizing had been carried out with this genus, but the last few years have witnessed an upsurge in the breeding of intergeneric hybrids from Australia. Zygopetalums have been crossed with *Colax* to produce *Zygocolax*, *Neogardneria* which gives *Zygoneria*, and with *Aganisia*, *Batemannia*, *Otostylis* and *Zygosepalum* which created the multigeneric hybrid *Hamelwellsara*. These new hybrids are increasing the range of highly fragrant, free flowering, modest-size orchids for the cool and intermediate greenhouses. The plants most frequently seen for sale are cool growing.

While these orchids are considered more of a challenge they are nevertheless well worth growing once you have gained some experience with easier types.

Temperature: Cool- to intermediate-growing.

Cultivation: Grow in pots or open slatted baskets of bark-based compost (growing medium). They require shady conditions for most of the year, and need to be watered more in the summer and less in the winter. Feed can be applied while they are growing. The foliage of zygopetalums is easily marked if water rests on the surface for too long. For this reason they are better not sprayed on a regular basis with water, but watered only through the roots. *Height*: 30–45cm (12–18in).

Zygopetalum Artur Elle 'Stonehurst'

The bold colours of the flowers, which are lime-green with deep purple spotting and have a purple lip, make this an unusual orchid for indoor cultivation. The plant blooms from the new growths in the early spring. Grow in a fairly cool room with good light, but out of direct sun.

Zygopetalum Artur Elle 'Stonehurst'

SPECIALIST ORCHIDS

The orchids described on the following pages can be grown alongside most of those already mentioned in order to add variety to any collection. All are intriguing plants, which you will grow to appreciate as they become more familiar.

ACINETA

Of the 15 species of *Acineta*, which all come from South America, only a few are in general cultivation. These evergreen epiphytic orchids produce stout, cone-shaped pseudobulbs with usually two, occasionally more, semi-rigid, broad leaves. The plants resemble the stanhopeas, being of a similar size at around 30cm (12in) tall. The flower spikes come from the base of the latest pseudobulb and develop over the rim of the container, eventually becoming pendent. The flowers, clustered on the spike, have a heavy, waxy texture and are strongly coloured. The plants bloom mostly during the summer.
Temperature: Intermediate-growing, with a minimum winter night temperature of 13°C (55°F).
Cultivation: Grow in hanging, open, slatted baskets in a coarse bark compost (growing medium), in good light all year round. Commence watering immediately new growth is seen, usually in the spring. During the growing season, water and apply feed at every other watering. Spray the foliage and maintain a good humidity. Allow the plants to rest when dormant during the winter.
Height: 30cm (12in).

Acineta superba
These robust orchids from South America need to grow in baskets to enable their downward-growing flower spikes to hang freely. The fragrant flowers, which appear in spring and summer, are cupped, with the smaller petals standing close to the lip.

Acineta superba

AERANGIS

There are about 50 species in this natural genus of monopodial orchids, which hail from Africa and Madagascar. The plants produce a fan-like assemblage of semi-rigid leaves that grow from a central rhizome. Most of the species resemble the phalaenopsis in habit, but their leaves are thicker. The flower spikes may bear from just one to numerous flowers on pendent spikes, over 30cm (12in) long. The flowers are mostly white, with a long spur at the back of the flower. This spur is an extension of the back of the lip, and is used by the flower to ensure pollination by a moth with a tongue of the same length. The white flowers are attractive to night-flying moths.

Limited hybridizing has been done with this genus, and intergeneric hybrids have been made crossing *Aerangis* with *Angraecum* (*Angrangis*) and others. When you look at the clear, natural beauty of these often pristine white blooms, it is difficult to see how hybridizing can improve upon them. The species are exquisite, and if you grow any of the orchids from this group, you will want to obtain as many as possible.

A greenhouse suits them best, where they can be suspended from the roof in open baskets to allow their flowers to be shown to their best advantage.
Temperature: Warm-growing.
Cultivation: Grow in a fine bark compost (growing medium) in slatted baskets in good light. Small species can also be mounted on bark. Keep them moist all year round and mist them regularly to maintain humidity. Feed lightly at every second watering. Leave plants undisturbed, but add a small amount of compost (growing medium) to the base of the plant from time to time. If on bark, add a wad of fibre or moss around the base.
Height: From 15cm (6in).

Aerangis luteo alba var. rhodostricta
This is an attractive dwarf species from parts of Africa, where it grows on twigs in dry, exposed areas. The plant is only a few inches high, and the white flowers, which appear in winter, have an unusually bright red column and are large in comparison.

Aerangis luteo-alba var. *rhodostricta*

ANGRAECUM

Related to the smaller-growing *Aerangis* are the lovely angraecums. These superb epiphytic, lithophytic or terrestrial orchids come from all over southern Africa and Madagascar. The monopodial plants vary in size, and, of the 200 or so species, many can be found in cultivation. Among the smallest is *Angraecum distichum*, a dwarf plant with plaited (braided), herringbone-like foliage, whose oval leaves overlap along a curving rhizome, which rarely exceeds 15cm (6in) in length. The minute flowers (5mm/¼in wide) are produced singly all over the plant, to resemble stars in a night sky. The giants of the genus include the magnificent *A. sesquipedale*. In between these extremes are further desirable and collectable species as well as a few hybrids.

These evergreen plants make attractive specimens, even when they are not in flower. Their blooms are produced mainly during the winter and spring, when they will last for several weeks.
Temperature: Intermediate-growing, with a minimum winter temperature of 13°C (55°F) at night.
Cultivation: Grow smaller angraecums in half pots or mounted on pieces of cork bark. The larger plants need to be grown in pots with an open, coarse compost (growing medium). As the temperature rises in summer, increase the humidity to maintain the balance. These are low-light plants, which need good shade in summer and filtered light in winter. Water all year round and apply feed, but give less to those in pots in winter because they will take longer to dry out.
Height: 15cm (6in) to over 30cm (12in).

Angraecum sesquipedale
The comet orchid from Madagascar is so called because of its extraordinarily long spur. The waxy, ivory-white flower is 15cm (6in) across, and the plant will grow to over 30cm (12in). Several flowers can be carried on one spike and appear in winter.

Angraecum sesquipedale

Bifrenaria harrisoniae

BIFRENARIA

About 30 species make up this natural genus of mainly epiphytic plants, which originate from Brazil, Peru and as far north as Panama. Several species are in cultivation, the most popular being *Bifrenaria harrisoniae*, with its strikingly beautiful colouring. This species can be grown with comparative ease and blooms regularly in late summer, thus making it an ideal orchid to grow, even for the relatively inexperienced orchid-grower.

Typically, the plants produce cone-shaped, yellowish to green pseudobulbs with a single, wide, ribbed leaf. The flowers are produced on short flower spikes that huddle below the foliage, bearing two or more flowers.

These orchids do well in a mixed collection, being easily accommodated among other plants. When they are large enough, the plants can be divided into smaller pieces, provided there is a new growth on each division. Alternatively, new plants can be grown from the backbulbs that are removed from the main plant at repotting time.
Temperature: Cool-growing.
Cultivation: Grow in 10cm (4in) pots in a fine bark compost (growing medium) in good light. Water and apply feed regularly during the summer growing season. The foliage can be lightly sprayed in summer while the plants are out of flower. Allow the plants to dry out while resting in winter. Water should be given during this time only if the plants shrivel.
Height: To 30cm (12in).

Bifrenaria harrisoniae
A most pleasing species for the cool greenhouse or indoors, the large flowers, 8cm (3in) wide, which bloom in early summer, are waxy, creamy white and have a deep mauve, hairy lip. One to two flowers are produced on a short spike below the leaves.

BULBOPHYLLUM

The bulbophyllums comprise a huge genus of upwards of 1,000 species, among which can be found some of the most extraordinary and outlandish flowers. The plants are extremely variable, ranging in size from tiny plants with little rounded, pea-size pseudobulbs (such as *Bulbophyllum roxburghii*) to the giants such as *B. fletcherianum*, whose ungainly flowers resemble the gaping mouths of baby birds. This plant has leaves that hang down over 30cm (12in), resembling the old-fashioned razor strops. In between are literally hundreds of species and a very few hybrids, all with amazing flowers. Some are decidedly ugly and have a strong odour reminiscent of carrion. Others are exceedingly pretty, while others produce flattened stems with beetle-like flowers, which typify one small group among this extremely diverse genus. All the plants are evergreen and epiphytic, some of the

Bulbophyllum barbigerum

smaller species being known as "twig epiphytes" because they cling to the very extremities of the smallest branches.

Bulbophyllums are widely distributed throughout South-east Asia as well as Africa, Australia and tropical America. They must be regarded as one of the most successful genera among the orchids. If you cannot recognize one orchid from a display at an orchid event, the chances are that it is a *Bulbophyllum*!

Try some of the smaller plants indoors, where they will do well in pots, baskets or on bark. The smaller species will grow with great vigour, multiplying their pseudobulbs each year until a large specimen plant is built up. When placed in a hanging basket, the plants can grow into huge leafy balls completely surrounding their container. The numerous flowering spikes that are produced will cover the plant to create a most eye-catching sight.

These are really fun orchids to grow, but watch out for the bad-smelling ones. Go instead for those gems with a rocking lip, such as *Bulbophyllum lobbii*, or those with the amazingly long sepals, such as *B. medusae*, or the alluring, tantalizingly mobile flowers of *B. barbigerum*. You will not be disappointed.
Temperature: Cool-growing (some are best in intermediate conditions).
Cultivation: Grow on bark or in pots or baskets of bark compost (growing medium). Water well in summer, but give less in winter. Do not allow those with small pseudobulbs to shrivel. Feed every second watering. Once established, give plenty of light, but avoid direct sunlight. In winter they need as much light as possible.
Height: 7–30cm (3–12in).

Bulbophyllum barbigerum
These tantalizing 1cm (½in) dark red flowers have a movable lip that is adorned with bristling hairs. The slightest movement causes them to wave in a way that is likely to attract a pollinator. The plant will remain in bloom for months.

Bulbophyllum dayanum

Bulbophyllum dayanum

This small plant, less than 15cm (6in) in height, produces its modest flowers in clusters around the base in summer. Each 5mm (¼in) bloom has short hairs to the edges of its sepals and petals and the lip is blood red. Its appearance is intended to mimic an open wound on an animal's hide.

Bulbophyllum purpureorachis

Among the bulbophyllums can be found some of the strangest flowers in the orchid family. This curious species from Africa carries its small, beetle-like flowers along two sides of a tall, flattened stem.

Bulbophyllum purpureoachis

CALANTHE

This is a genus of about 150 terrestrial species spread through parts of Asia. Of these, only a handful of species and hybrids are in general cultivation.

The genus can be divided into two distinct groups. The first, which is more widely grown, contains deciduous plants that have large, silvery pseudobulbs and wide, spreading, ribbed leaves. They are short-lived and die in their second year, The flowers – mainly pink and white – are spread along a tall, arching flower spike, which emerges from the base of the leafless pseudobulb during the autumn and winter, while the plant is at rest. Modern hybridizing within this group has resulted in some highly desirable deep red clones. The flower stems are soft and hairy, and the blooms have a delicate appeal.

The second group are the evergreen types. These come mainly from across China and Japan and are highly regarded by the Japanese, who grow them to perfection, creating new hybrids along the way. This group produces small, diminutive pseudobulbs with wide, spreading foliage. The flower

Calanthe **Baron Schroder**

Calanthe Corbiere

Calanthe Gorey × Grouville

spikes come from the base, and carry numerous colourful flowers with yellow, pink, white and green being popular.

Calanthes have a short, fast-growing season. Because of the speed at which they grow, these are really exciting orchids to cultivate, but they do need plenty of headroom while in leaf. Repot each spring when the growth starts. If the oldest pseudobulb is dead and shrivelled, remove it; if it is still firm and plump, it may be potted separately to give you two new plants next season.

Temperature: Intermediate-growing, with a minimum temperature of 16°C (60°F) at night.
Cultivation: Grow in pots of a terrestrial orchid mix containing some peat and perlite. Begin watering and feeding as soon as new growth is seen in the spring. While in growth, the plants should be kept well shaded. Too much humidity, as well as spraying of the leaves, can cause the foliage to spot. This is not a great problem because it is shed in autumn, after turning yellow. At this time, reduce the watering

and discontinue for the winter while the flower spike is extending and the flowering period lasts. After flowering, remove the plants to a position in full light, but take care to retrieve them as soon as you see the new growth the next year.
Height: To 1m (3ft) when in leaf.

Calanthe Baron Schroder
One of the older hybrids among the genus raised in 1894, this plant produces its pink and white flowers over many months in winter and spring. The silvery pseudobulbs can be up to 15cm (6in) high. In summer, the plants are in leaf and need plenty of headroom in a warm greenhouse.

Calanthe Corbiere
This milk-white hybrid is from the group of deciduous calanthes produced from *Calanthe* Harrisii. These plants bloom during the winter and spring while the plant is dormant.

Calanthe Gorey × Grouville
Numerous flowers are produced over an extended period during the winter. Over 2.5cm (1in) wide, they are carried on a very tall flower spike that can grow to over 1m (3ft) as it develops.

CIRRHOPETALUM

While some authorities consider all cirrhopetalums as part of the huge, closely related genus *Bulbophyllum*, others keep them distinct. There are obvious similarities between the plants, which often cannot be distinguished out of bloom, but the flowers can be horticulturally recognized by the extremely long and tapering sepals produced by the majority of the species. They are mentioned here as a separate genus firstly because the older name is retained for horticultural usage and secondly to enable the reader to distinguish readily between them. For hybrid registration purposes, both *Bulbophyllum* and *Cirrhopetalum* have been recognized, with four bigeneric hybrids being registered as *Cirrhophyllum* in 1965.

Culturally, cirrhopetalums require the same conditions and treatment as bulbophyllums. The species exhibit their twirling flowers in close umbels at the end of slender flower spikes. The overall effect of the closely aligned flowers, with stumpy petals touching and the elegantly tapering sepals forming a distinct waterfall, is quite captivating. The colours can be strong, with red being the main colour. The small, often glossy or wet-looking, projecting lip attracts flies on the lookout for raw meat.

Cirrhopetalum rothschildianum carries a fringe of small hairs on the tips of the petals and dorsal sepal like an exclamation mark, creating an alien air.

Temperature: Cool-growing (some are best in intermediate conditions).

Cultivation: Grow on bark or in pots or baskets of bark compost (growing medium). Water well in summer, but give less in winter. Do not allow those with small pseudobulbs to shrivel. Feed every second watering. Once established, give plenty of light, but avoid direct sunlight. In winter they need as much light as possible.

Height: 15cm (6in).

Cirrhopetalum Elizabeth Ann 'Bucklebury' AM/RHS
This is one of only a few exciting hybrids to be produced from this genus. The flowers, which appear at various times, extend their long, tapering sepals for several centimetres (inches), and the dorsals are adorned with small tufts of hairs.

Cirrhopetalum guttulatum
In winter and spring, little flowers less than 1cm (½in) wide adorn this pretty, easily grown and flowered species, which does well indoors or in a cool greenhouse. The flower spikes are under 15cm (6in) tall.

Cirrhopetalum umbellatum
A robust species with plants over 15cm (6in) tall, this has drooping flower spikes that terminate in umbels of large flowers where the sepals are extended to form the edge of the ring. The petals and lip are very small. The flowers bloom in spring.

Cirrhopetalum guttulatum

Cirrhopetalum umbellatum

Cirrhopetalum Elizabeth Ann 'Bucklebury' AM/RHS

CYRTOCHILUM

This genus contains about 150 evergreen epiphytic species, which originate from South and Central America, often at high elevations in the Andes. The plants were at one time included in the genus *Oncidium*, but are now considered distinct, although the latter name persists in orchid-growing circles. Very few of the species, and virtually no hybrids, are cultivated. Mostly the species are rare and much treasured. The main appreciable difference between *Cyrtochilum* and *Oncidium* is the size of the lip, which, so often exaggerated in the oncidiums, is much reduced in favour of broad, spreading sepals in the cyrtochilums.

The plants, which can be over 30cm (12in) tall, produce robust pseudobulbs with narrowly oval leaves. Typically, the flower spikes are extremely long, often reaching 4–5m (12–16½ft) in length. The flowers are spread out, appearing in little clusters along most of their length. These long flower spikes can be trained into a hoop, which makes accommodating them easier and enables the flowers to be seen more clearly.

Cyrtochilums do well alongside other members of the *Odontoglossum* alliance. Some of the species produce their new pseudobulbs along an upward-creeping rhizome, with a long gap in between. One good way of growing these is to insert a mossy pole into a heavy flowerpot and allow the plant to extend upwards. Aerial roots soon become a feature of these plants.

Temperature: Cool-growing.

Cultivation: Grow in 10cm (4in) pots in a coarse bark compost (growing medium) or insert a moss-covered pole in the pot for the orchid to climb up. Provide shade during the summer and give more light in winter. Water throughout the year, but give less in winter. Apply feed in summer at every other watering.

Height: 60cm (2ft).

Cyrtochilum annulares

Clusters of chocolate-brown, yellow-edged flowers are produced in summer at intervals along an extremely long stem, which is best trained into a hoop.

Cyrtochilum annulares

DENDROCHILUM

Dendrochilums are evergreen epiphytic orchids, which come from the continent of Asia, but are also found in the Philippines and New Guinea. Of the 120 or so species, very few are generally grown, and there appear to be no hybrids. This rarity in cultivation reflects the plants' scarcity in the wild, and it is possible that they have never been that abundant.

The plants are neat, with evergreen pseudobulbs and a single, narrow, oval leaf, seldom reaching more than 25cm (10in) tall. The slender flower spikes come from the base of the new growth, and most are autumn-flowering. When grown on into large specimen plants, their sight and fragrance is not something to be forgotten, for these are among the prettiest of little orchid flowers.

Do not be tempted to divide these orchids until absolutely necessary: the larger the plant, the better they look.

The common name for these delightful, modestly sized orchids is silver chain orchids, or in some instances golden chain orchids. This refers to the slender flower spike, which is densely packed with small, white or yellow flowers, arranged in two distinct rows along most of its length.

Temperature: Cool-growing.

Cultivation: Grow in pots or hanging baskets of fine bark compost (growing

Dendrochilum cobbianum

Dendrochilum glumaceum

medium). Provide shady conditions when in growth, but full light during the winter. Water all year, but give much less during the winter while the plants are resting. Feed only in summer, at every other watering.

Height: 23cm (9in).

Dendrochilum cobbianum

This sweetly scented, cool-growing species from the Philippines, which grows to about 30cm (12in) tall, carries hundreds of small, white flowers on drooping spikes. It blooms in early summer and is suitable for indoor or greenhouse culture.

Dendrochilum glumaceum

An easily grown species, this blooms freely during the early summer with cascading sprays of small, whitish flowers with orange lips, densely packed in a herringbone pattern along the flower spike. The flowers carry a very strong, attractive scent.

EULOPHIA

Over 200 species of *Eulophia* are distributed throughout the African continent. These are terrestrial orchids, which produce large pseudobulbs from a strong rhizome, with wide, spreading leaves. The flower spikes come from the base of the newly completed pseudobulb. The genus is extremely varied, and plants of differing sizes are found, although not many are in general cultivation. In their natural state, these orchids may exist in wet marshland or on dry and arid hillsides. Their different cultural requirements may be one reason for their lack of popularity in cultivation. Nevertheless, these are excellent plants to grow and not all are space-consuming giants.

An interesting feature of some of the species is the unusual flower shape: the petals turn on a flat plane, possibly offering a wider landing platform for insects.

These are specialist plants, whose requirements need to be addressed for successful cultivation.
Temperature: Cool- or intermediate-growing, depending upon the species.
Cultivation: Pot in an open coarse mix of chunky bark and peat, to which has been added a portion of perlite. Water and feed while in active growth. Water or rest in winter according to its natural habitat (only water if the plant is in active growth).
Height: 30cm (12in).

Eulophia euglossa
An unusual terrestrial species from Africa, this produces slender, leafy pseudobulbs and showy flowers on an upright spike in summer. The pointed blooms are apple green with a white lip.

Eulophia euglossa

GONGORA

This is a small, natural genus of about 25 species, a number of which are cultivated, mostly by specialist growers mesmerized by the small, curiously formed flowers. A plant in bloom most often conjures up images of birds in flight, or, occasionally, insects flying in formation. There are no hybrids, probably because the species offer all that anyone could require from this type of orchid.

Closely related to the stanhopeas, the gongoras are mainly smaller plants with ribbed, cone-shaped, green pseudobulbs, supporting a pair of narrowly oval to wide leaves. The flower spikes come from the base of the newly completed pseudobulbs in the early summer, and some are extremely fragrant. The spikes hang around the edge of the plant's container, often in profusion. These evergreen epiphytic species hail mostly from Brazil, with others coming from Peru and further north to Mexico.

Further fanciful attempts to describe the flowers have given rise to the name of Punch and Judy orchid: turn one flower on its side and see the two quarrelling figures appear to be battling it out with each other!

Although not plentiful in cultivation, these orchids are well worth growing, but need to be bought from specialist nurseries.
Temperature: Cool- to intermediate-growing.
Cultivation: Grow in pots or in hanging baskets in fine bark compost (growing medium). Give shade in summer, and full light in winter. Water and apply feed throughout the summer. Water sparingly during the winter to keep the pseudobulbs plump.
Height: 23cm (9in).

Gongora maculata
Among the strangest of flowers produced by any orchid, this species from tropical America projects a cascade of flowers, 4cm (1½in) long, like birds in flight, from the base of the pseudobulb in summer. It is lightly scented.

Gongora maculata

Jumellia sagittata

JUMELLIA

Coming mainly from Madagascar, these monopodial, clump-forming, evergreen epiphytic plants resemble angraecums in their growth, which is robust, with long, fleshy leaves. Of the 40 or so species, only a very few are grown, none of which is plentiful in cultivation, and the genus has not produced any hybrids except for a very few intergenerics with related genera such as *Angraecum* and *Aeranthes* (syn. *Angranthellea*).

The flowers, which are disappointingly small for the size of the plant, are produced on slender flower spikes and are typically solely white, with sepals, petals and a lip of equal proportions. This structure as well as the presence of a long spur indicates pollination by night-flying moths, which means that the flower has no need of other coloration or indeed fragrance.

Temperature: Warm-growing.

Cultivation: Grow in 15cm (6in) pots or baskets containing a coarse, chunky compost (growing medium) to accommodate the long roots, which often meander at will. Provide shade and high humidity, as for *Phalaenopsis*. Water and feed throughout the year, giving less in winter.

Height: 45cm (18in).

Jumellia sagittata

A robust-growing species from Madagascar, this produces *Vanda*-like growth. The flowers, 4cm (1½in) wide, are carried singly on spindly spikes that are shorter than the height of the plant. A profusion of blooms crowds around the base in winter.

LOCKHARTIA

Lockhartias are not common in cultivation, and of the 30 or so evergreen epiphytic species endemic to Mexico and nearby, only a very few are grown. The plants are nevertheless interesting, having distinct foliage that forms two ranks along the entire length of the erect stems. The flowers, which are small and yellow, not unlike *Oncidium*, appear in groups from between the leaves at intervals along the stem.

These orchids have a fine rooting system that will quickly adhere to any bark surface, provided there is sufficient moisture. They do not have a noticeable dormant period but will slow their growth during the winter months.
Temperature: Intermediate-growing.
Cultivation: Grow in small pots of fine bark compost (growing medium) or mounted on bark. Spray regularly during summer to keep the foliage from dehydrating. Water all year, and apply feed lightly during the summer.
Height: To 30cm (12in).

Lockhartia oerstedii
This species produces leafy stems, up to 30cm (12in) tall. The small, overlapping leaves create an unusual plaited appearance. The small, bright yellow flowers are produced over a period of several weeks in summer.

Lockhartia oerstedii

Ludisia discolor

LUDISIA

Members of this genus of attractive terrestrials, which originate from China, are known as jewel orchids. This is one of a very few orchid genera that are cultivated for their foliage rather than for their flowers. The leaves of this pretty orchid are exquisite: dark velvety green is overlaid with silver and gold veining in intricate lines all over the leaf surface. At night, shine a torch on to the leaves and see them glisten; the same effect is achieved by allowing the sun to shine momentarily upon them. But these are essentially shade-loving plants, used to growing as terrestrials or lithophytes along the banks of rivers and streams where the light is poor and the sun seldom filters down. In their native home across India and China, they grow upon mossy rocks close to water, but they often do well indoors, where the drier atmosphere suits them.

The plants produce rosettes of leaves at intervals along a creeping rhizome. Shortly after the appearance of the new growth, roots appear around the base and these will penetrate the compost (growing medium). The flowers appear from the centre of the maturing growth on an upright flower spike. The curious, pretty blooms are white with yellow on the lip. A large plant that has been allowed to grow on, producing multiple growths, will create a lasting impression, with numerous flower spikes open all at once.
Temperature: Warm-growing.
Cultivation: Grow in pans with an open, gritty compost (growing medium) suitable for terrestrial orchids. Keep well shaded all year. Keep evenly moist. If the plants become overwet at any time, rotting is quick to follow. Water carefully in summer and sparingly during the winter. Feed the plants lightly at every third watering.
Height: 15cm (6in).

Ludisia discolor
This species is grown for its beautiful, velvety, dark green and veined foliage. It is a terrestrial plant that blooms from the centre of the growth, producing flower spikes, about 30cm (12in) tall, of delightfully curious white flowers. The flowers bloom in summer.

MEXICOA

This genus contains just one species, which has been moved from *Oncidium* and given monotypic status. *Mexicoa ghiesbrechtiana* is small in stature, with oval pseudobulbs and a pair of narrowly oval leaves. As its name suggests, it originates from Mexico and grows epiphytically. This is an ideal subject for inclusion in a collection of miniature orchids, since this little plant rarely exceeds 15cm (6in) in height, even when in flower. It associates well with other members of the *Odontoglossum* alliance. The attractive blooms, on short flower spikes, are yellow and the petals and sepals are shaded with brown. The lip is large, reminiscent of *Oncidium*, and dominates the flower. The flowers appear mainly during summer and will last for a few weeks.

Temperature: Cool-growing.
Cultivation: Grow in pots of fine bark compost (growing medium) or mounted on bark. Grow in good shade in summer, but give more light in winter. Water all year, but give less in winter. Feed lightly at every third watering in summer. Lightly mist the foliage in summer.
Height: To 15cm (6in).

Mexicoa ghiesbrechtiana

A delightful miniature species from Mexico, this requires a cool situation. The plants are no more than 15cm (6in) tall and the pretty flowers, which come on arching spikes, are yellow and brown. The lip is large and flared. The plant blooms mainly during the summer.

Mexicoa ghiesbrechtiana

MILTONIA

There are about ten species of *Miltonia* and very few pure hybrids. The genus was divided from *Miltoniopsis*, the true pansy orchids, the notable difference being the lack of the large, flat lip, and the distribution of the plants. Miltonias are confined to Brazil, whereas miltoniopsis are spread mainly throughout Colombia. Some confusion can arise when the incorrect name is used for miltoniopsis, where, for hybrid registration purposes, *Miltonia* is retained.

Miltonias are evergreen epiphytes with neat, green pseudobulbs, often produced along a creeping rhizome. The flowers come from the base of the new growth and are spread along an arching or upright flower spike. The flowers are variable, and the most spectacular have been used for hybridizing with other related members of the *Odontoglossum* alliance.

Temperature: Warm-growing.
Cultivation: Grow those that produce their pseudobulbs at intervals along a rhizome in half-pots or baskets of a shape that easily accommodates their elongated outline, using a bark-based compost (growing medium). Give good shade in summer, but more light in winter. Feed at every other watering in summer, and maintain a good humidity.
Height: 23cm (9in).

Miltonia confusa (syn. *Miltonioides confusa*)
This lovely fragrant species from Costa Rica produces its eye-catching, red and green flowers mainly during the winter and spring. The flowers are long-lasting.

Miltonia flavescens
Suitable for warm growing, this species has slender pseudobulbs and numerous pale-coloured flowers on a spike. It will last for several weeks during the summer.

Miltonia confusa

Miltonia warscewiczii
(syn. *Miltonioides warscewiczii*)
This warm-growing species is unusual for the "window" of almost translucent tissue that can be seen in the middle of the lip. The flowers, which appear in early summer, are cherry red. Some handsome hybrids have been raised from this species.

Miltonia warscewiczii var. alba
(syn. *Miltonioides warscewiczii* var. *alba*)
The albino form of the species, which comes from South America, has near-white flowers in early summer, and is quite rare. It carries fewer flowers on the spike than the type. This plant does best when grown in a warm greenhouse.

Miltonia warscewiczii

Miltonia flavescens

Miltonia warscewiczii var. *alba*

NEOFINETA

Neofineta has been settled upon a single species, which has undergone numerous name changes since its discovery in 1784. It is a small-growing, monopodial, evergreen species from Japan, which has a large following of devoted growers who cultivate the plant for its often-seen, variegated foliage, considered in Japan to be highly decorative. The plant seldom reaches more than 10cm (4in) in height, producing semi-rigid, fleshy leaves from the apex. The flowers, usually two or three on a short stem, are white with a long, curving spur.

Temperature: Cool-growing.
Cultivation: Grow in a small container of fine bark compost (growing medium) or mounted on bark. Maintain good light and high humidity by spraying the foliage regularly. Keep moist all year, and apply feed during the summer.
Height: To 10cm (4in).

Neofineta falcata

This is an attractive, modestly sized, monopodial plant with flower spikes of pure white blooms, each with a long spur. Grow in good light in a cool greenhouse. Flowers appear at various times.

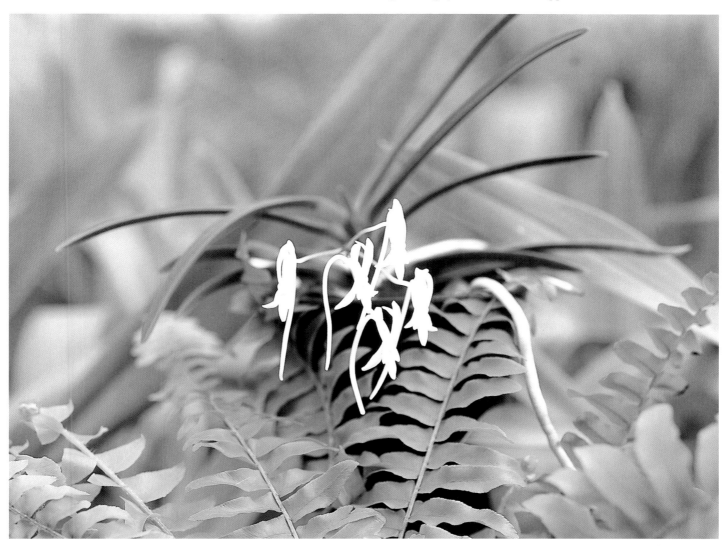

Neofineta falcata

PLEUROTHALLIS

This is one natural genus among several that comprise a huge alliance of miniature orchids, known as the Pleurothallidinae alliance. These often tiny, always delightful, orchids have a large following of devoted growers, and specialist societies are confined entirely to the promotion of this group. Among these can be found some of the smallest orchids in the world, which need the assistance of an eye glass in order to study their tiny but intricate flowers.

There are considered to be about 900 species distributed throughout Central and South America. Some have been transferred to separate genera, but often appear under the older name in cultivation. Many of these are grown, but little hybridizng has been attempted.

Various sections within the genus are characterized by the habit of the plant. Notable are those with short, slender stems that support a single wide leaf. The flowers appear at the apex and "sit" on the leaf surface, resembling a little beetle, as with *Pleurothallis matuadina*. Others deliver an explosion of minute flowers from the leaf axil, as with *P. octomerioides*. Yet others produce leafy stems, their cotton-thin flower spikes coming from near the base and carrying several tiny flowers on stems only just taller than the foliage. Some of the smallest, such as *P. grobyi*, compare with the giants of the genus, including the dark, brooding flowers of *P. roezlii*.

Pleurothallis are extremely easy plants to grow, and large specimens can be attained with a few years of growing. They flower freely, and those that produce sequential flowerings will continue to flower for months.
Temperature: Cool-growing.
Cultivation: Grow in pots of fine bark compost (growing medium). Keep shaded in summer, and admit full light in winter. Water all year, but give less in winter. Feed lightly at every third watering.
Height: 5–23cm (2–9in).

Pleurothallis peduncularis
From a huge genus of often minuscule orchids comes this little plant, whose tiny blooms explode from the base of the leaf in early autumn. These are off-white, with a tiny, jewel-like lip at the centre.

ROSSIOGLOSSUM

At one time grouped with the odontoglossums, this magnificent genus has been afforded separate status. The evergreen epiphytic plants come from Central America, where six species have been identified. All are highly desirable plants, not at all common in cultivation. Although defined as members of the *Odontoglossum* alliance, rossioglossums will not cross breed with any other genus; in fact, they are extremely difficult to hybridize within their own select genus. As a result, there are very few hybrids available.

The plants have dark green pseudobulbs and a pair of dark green, oval leaves that are peppered with brown when the new growth is young. This unusual feature is often mistaken for insect infestation. The flower spikes come from the base of the new growth in the autumn and produce several flowers on a stem. These are mostly large, strongly coloured flowers, typically yellow and red-brown. The plants commence their new growths late in the year, and it is often early summer before these show.

Rossioglossum **Rawdon Jester**

Pleurothallis peduncularis

Temperature: Cool-growing.
Cultivation: Grow in 10cm (4in) pots of bark-based compost (growing medium). Shade in summer, but allow full light in winter. Water while the plants are in growth, decreasing gradually as the pseudobulbs mature. When no growth is visible, allow the plants to remain dry but without undue shrivelling of the pseudobulb. Feed at every other watering in summer.
Height: 23cm (9in).

Rossioglossum Rawdon Jester

This is the only successful hybrid in a genus that is extremely reluctant to produce seed or hybridize. The striking, huge flowers, 12cm (5in) wide, are boldly coloured in chestnut brown and yellow. The flowers appear in autumn and winter. This hybrid will grow indoors or in a cool greenhouse.

SARCOCHILUS

This is a small, monopodial genus of modestly sized plants that come from Australia. Of the 15 or so species, only a very few are seen in cultivation. These, and one hybrid, grow with comparative ease, and excellent specimens are seen which are an indication of the plants' reliability. These mostly epiphytic plants produce pairs of semi-rigid leaves on stems that do not become too tall. New growth is produced from the base. In this way, a tufted plant is created that will bloom profusely during the winter months. The flowers, held on upright flower spikes, are white with red circular spotting at the centre.

Temperature: Intermediate-growing.
Cultivation: Grow in 5–10cm (2–4in) pots of fine bark compost (growing medium). Shade in summer, but provide more light in winter. Water all year; feed in summer at every other watering.
Height: 15cm (6in).

Sarcochilus Fitzhart

This is an attractive primary hybrid between two species, *Sarcochilus fitzgeraldii* and *S. hartmannii*, from Australia. The plant produces tufted growths, and blooms freely in spring on flower spikes held well above the foliage. The petite, rounded flowers are white with a central red marking.

Sarcochilus **Fitzhart**

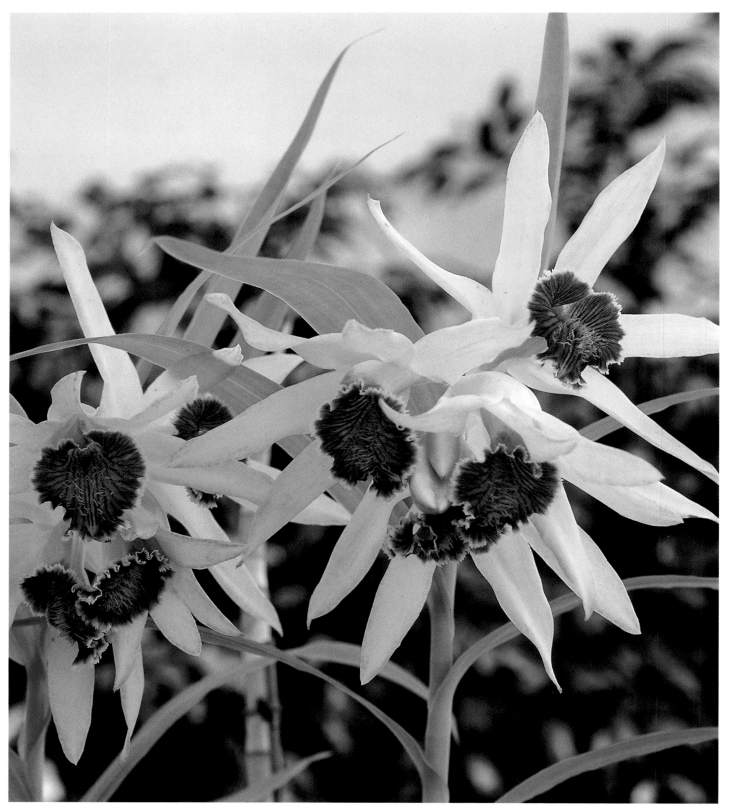

Thunia **Gattonense**

THUNIA

A few species make up this small genus of beautiful orchids from India. These, and one very old hybrid that has stood the test of time, make superb-looking plants in summer with tall, fleshy stems softly leafed along their length. When mature, they will reach 60cm (2ft) or more. The papery flowers appear in a frothy cascade at the apex of the stem and last for about three weeks in summer. These are usually white, with yellow or pinky red on the lip.

Thunias are very exciting plants to grow. From the moment the new growth is seen in early spring, they race forward at a great pace, completing their season's growth in record time, so that by early summer, growth is complete and the flower spikes are showing.

The canes are short-lived, and shrivel and die after one year. In autumn, the plants shed their foliage, which turns from green to golden yellow before being discarded. When this happens, take the bare canes out of the pot and place them in a seed tray in full light. Leave them completely dry for the winter. In spring, remove the old dead canes, and pot up the plump ones when you see the new growths.

Temperature: Cool- to intermediate-growing (the warmer you grow them, the earlier in the year thunias will bloom).
Cultivation: Grow in 10cm (4in) pots of bark-based compost (growing medium), or try growing in Rockwool. Water well once the roots have started, and feed, but keep the foliage dry to avoid spotting. Keep dry in winter. Keep in shade all summer, but give full light in winter.
Height: To 60cm (2ft) or more.

Thunia **Gattonense**

A old classic hybrid raised 100 years ago, this is a delightful plant to grow, with beautiful foliage and large, frothing heads of flowers, 10cm (4in) across, in summer.

TRICHOPILIA

Of the 30 or so species in this evergreen epiphytic genus, which occurs in Central and South America, only a few are occasionally seen in cultivation. There are no hybrids within this genus, which is a pity because those species that are grown have much to commend them, and hybridizing could possibly combine their separate qualities.

The plants are modestly sized, fitting nicely into a mixed collection indoors or in a cool greenhouse. Most do not exceed 15cm (6in) in height, with flower spikes below the foliage, often drooping. The petals and sepals of *Trichopilia tortilis* are long and narrow, twisting along their length, which gives rise to the common name, corkscrew orchid. This, and others in cultivation, are extremely pretty and easy to grow and flower. The plants bloom in late summer or autumn and last for a few weeks. They are seen at their best when grown on into specimen plants but, if preferred, they may be divided when large enough to maintain them at a desired size.

Temperature: Cool-growing.
Cultivation: While most do well in pots of fine bark compost (growing medium), they can also be grown mounted on bark or other suitable bases. Water all year, but give less in winter while the plants are resting. Keep shaded in summer, and give more light in winter. Feed lightly in summer.
Height: To 15cm (6in).

Trichopilia tortilis

This corkscrew orchid has distinctive, twisting sepals and petals, which are long and narrow. The large, flared lip is white with some pink at the centre. The flowers are carried singly on drooping spikes during the summer.

Trichopilia tortilis

TEMPERATE TERRESTRIAL ORCHIDS

The following terrestrial orchids can be artificially raised from seed, and are sometimes available from hardy plant nurseries, while in growth and flower. Many more can be found in the wild, where they are all protected plants.

ANACAMPTIS

Although just two species make up this genus of European terrestrial orchids, only one is generally seen. This is the pyramidal orchid (*Anacamptis pyramidalis*), which occurs in abundance in parts of Britain, usually on dry hillsides and areas close to the sea. The name is derived from the shape of the inflorescence, which is densely packed with pretty, pale pink flowers. A white form is occasionally seen.

The plant, which also occurs in parts of Africa, blooms in early summer, after which it dies down, leaving a head of seed capsules.

Temperature: 1–5°C (34–41°F).
Cultivation: Grow in pots of coarse grit and leaf mould or a similar compost (growing medium) in a frost-free greenhouse or cold frame. Water while in active growth. Keep dry in winter. Alternatively, plant out in beds in well-drained situations. Allow to spread and leave undisturbed so they will colonize.
Height: 10cm (4in).

DACTYLORHIZA

Closely related to the genus *Orchis*, there are about 40 species spread throughout Europe, Asia and elsewhere. In Britain, this is a widespread and commonly seen genus, with plants covering large areas in marshy or boggy places. One of the largest species occurring in Africa is *Dactylorhiza foliosa*, and this can be seen in long-established colonies in botanical gardens. When planted out and left undisturbed, this species, and others, can be cultivated.

Dactylorhiza foliosa

The plants produce leafy stems that terminate in the flower spike. Dactylorhizas will often hybridize within a colony, making it difficult to determine the true species, which can be highly variable, giving rise to several distinct colour forms from white, through pale pink to deep mauve.
Temperature: 1–5°C (34–41°F).
Cultivation: Grow in pots of coarse grit and leaf mould or a similar compost (growing medium) in a frost-free greenhouse or cold frame. Water while in active growth. Keep dry in winter. Alternatively, plant out in beds in well-drained situations. Allow to spread and leave undisturbed so they will colonize.
Height: 10cm (4in) or larger.

Anacamptis pyramidalis

Ophrys apifera

Orchis mascula

OPHRYS

Of all the terrestrial orchids native to Europe, the ophrys are perhaps the most intriguing for the shape of their flowers and their mimicry of the insects that pollinate them. Fly orchid (*Ophrys insectifera*), spider orchid (*O. sphegodes*) and bee orchid (*O. apifera*) give some idea of the adaptation of the lips of the flowers to resemble the male pollinator, which is duped into attempted copulation with the flower, thus resulting in pollination. Of the 30 or so species that have been identified, there exist numerous sub-species, varieties and colour variations, which can make positive identification difficult.

While the majority of the species are found in the Mediterranean region, some can be seen in Britain, especially in coastal areas and grassland. In recent years, they have been successfully cultivated in pots.
Temperature: 1–5°C (34–41°F).
Cultivation: Grow in pots of coarse grit and leaf mould or a similar compost (growing medium) in a frost-free

greenhouse or cold frame. Water while in active growth. Keep dry in winter. Alternatively, plant out in beds in well-drained situations. Allow to spread and leave undisturbed so they will colonize.
Height: 5cm (2in).

ORCHIS

This attractive genus of terrestrial European orchids contains about 30 species spread throughout Europe and extending their range into North Africa and western Asia. In Britain, the early purple orchid (*Orchis mascula*) is the first of the native orchids to bloom, in late spring. Among this genus are some apt descriptions of their common names, which include the military orchid (*O. militaris*), named for the soldier-like appearance of the lip topped by a "helmet" of sepals and petals, and the monkey orchid (*O. simia*), whose extraordinary lip perfectly mimics the shape of a monkey. These species are extremely rare in Britain, but may be seen in profusion in other parts of Europe. Protected from disturbance in the wild, they are not cultivated in gardens.

These orchids rely heavily upon the mycorrhizal association with their own specific fungus, and their colonies can vary in number from year to year. The foliage appears in spring and forms a rosette of leaves from the centre of which extends the flower spike. Most *Orchis* favour dry meadows or heathland sites.
Temperature: 1–5°C (34–41°F).
Cultivation: Grow in pots of coarse grit and leaf mould or a similar compost (growing medium) in a frost-free greenhouse or cold frame. Water while in active growth. Keep dry in winter. Alternatively, plant out in beds in well-drained situations. Allow to spread and leave undisturbed so they will colonize.
Height: 16cm (6in) or larger.

PLATANTHERA

It is thought that there are about 100 species of this widely distributed orchid, which appears naturally across Europe, North America and elsewhere. The plants have widespread leaves and produce their flowers on a tall, upright flower spike. These are mostly white with a long spur, and are pollinated by night-flying hawk-moths. With the decline of their natural habitats of old pasture or land that has not been used extensively for agriculture, these orchids, once numerous, have dwindled in number. The greater butterfly orchid (*Platanthera chlorantha*) produces greenish white flowers, 30cm (12in) tall, on spikes which arise from two rounded, green leaves in early summer.
Temperature: 1–5°C (34–41°F).
Cultivation: Grow in pots of coarse grit and leaf mould or a similar compost (growing medium) in a frost-free greenhouse or cold frame. Water while in active growth. Keep dry in winter. Alternatively, plant out in beds in well-drained situations. Allow to spread and leave undisturbed so they will colonize.
Height: 15cm (6in) or larger.

Platanthera chlorantha

USEFUL ADDRESSES

EUROPE

Orchid Organizations

British Orchid Growers' Association
38 Florence Road, College Town
Sandhurst, Berkshire GU47 0QD
Tel: 01276 32947
Contact Mrs. Janet Plested

Orchid Society of Great Britain
10 Willoughby Close
Helpringham
Sleasford, Lincolnshire NG34 0RX
Tel: 01529 421521
Contact Mrs. Mary Smallman

Nurseries

Burnham Nurseries Ltd.
Forches Cross
Newton Abbot
Devon TQ12 6PZ
Tel: 01626 352233
Fax: 01626 362167
Email: burnhamorchids@eclipse.co.uk

David Stead Orchids
Greenscapes Horticultural Centre
Brandon Crescent
Shadwell
Leeds LS17 6JH
Tel/Fax: 0113 2893933

Deva Orchids
Littlebrook Farm
Stryt Isa
Pen-y-ffordd
Chester CH4 OJY
Tel: 01978 762454

Equatorial Plant Company
7 Gray Lane
Barnard Castle
County Durham DL12 8PD
Tel/Fax: 01833 690519
Email:
equatorialplants@onyx.net.co.uk

Ivans Orchids
Great Barn Dell
St. Albans Road
Sandridge, St. Albans
Hertfordshire AL4 9LB
Tel: 01727 863178
Fax: 01727 858545

Kenntner Orchideenzucht
D- 89555 Steinheim-Sontheim/St.
Birkelweg 12
Germany
Tel: 073 29/55 88
Fax: 073 29/1576

Mae Tang Tours
27 Blacon Point Road
Chester
Cheshire CH1 5LD
Tel: 01244 372479
Contact Mr. Peter Williams

McBean's Orchids
Cooksbridge
Lewes
East Sussex BN8 4PR
Tel: 01273 400228
Fax: 01273 401181

Miltoniopsis Jersey

Orchid Answers Ltd.
113 Second Avenue
Almodington
Birdham
Chichester
West Sussex PO20 7LF
Tel: 01243 511322
Fax: 01243 511474

Vacherot and Lecoufle
La Tuilerie
29 Rue de Valenton
94470 Boissy-Saint-Leger
France
Tel: (1) 45 69 10 42
Fax: (1) 45 98 30 14

Greenhouse and Equipment Suppliers
C H Whitehouse Ltd.
Dept J
Buckhurst Works
Bells Yew Green
Frant, Tunbridge Wells
Kent TN3 9BN
Tel: 01892 750247

Simply Control
139 Commercial Centre (BOG99)
Picket Place
Andover
Hampshire SP11 6RU
Tel: 01264 334805 (24 hours)
Fax: 01264 335755

UNITED STATES

Orchid Organizations
The American Orchid Society
6000 South Olive Avenue
West Palm Beach
FL 33405
Tel: (561) 585-8666
Tel: (561) 585-0654
Email: TheAOS@compuserve.com
www.orchidweb.org

Miltoniopsis **Marie Riopelle 'Portland Rose'**

Nurseries
Cal-Orchid, Inc.
1251 Orchid Drive
Santa Barbara, CA 93111
Tel: (805) 967-1312
Fax: (805) 967-6882

Carter and Holmes Orchids
629 Mendenhall Road
PO Box 668
Newberry, SC 29108
Tel: (803) 276-0579
Fax: (803) 276-0588
Email:
orchids@carterandholmes.com

Orchids by Hausermann Inc.
2N134 Addison Road
Villa Park
Illinois 60181-1191
Tel: (630) 543-6855
Fax: (630) 543-9842
Email: hausermann@compuserve.com
www.orchidsbyhausermann.com

AUSTRALIA

Nurseries
Adelaide Orchids
16 Pine Road
Woodcroft
South Australia 5162
Tel: 61 8 83812011
Fax: 61 8 83221546
Email: stephen@adelaideorchids.com
Internet home page:
http://www.adelaideorchids.com

Warrnambol Orchids
32 Riverside Terrace
Warrnambol 3280
Victoria
Tel: 613 556 2373
Fax: 613 556 12433
Email: altmann@standard.net.au
http://www.standard.net.au/-altman

INDEX

Page numbers in *italics* refer to illustrations.

Miltonia spectabilis **var.** *moreliana*

Zygopetalum maxillare

Laeliocattleya Chit Chat 'Tangerine'

Cymbidium Mini Ice 'Antarctic'

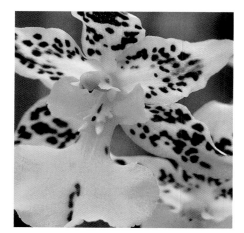

Odontocidium Isler's Gold Dragon

ACKNOWLEDGEMENTS

All special photography in this book was provided by Derek Cranch, except for the following:

KEY:- t = top   b = bottom   c = centre   r = right   l = left

Peter Anderson: 9t; 18bl; 43tl and tr; 67; 76t; 91tc.

Helen Fickling: 20 (all); 21; 34bl; 36; 38b; 39b; 41t; 42br; 77bl and br; 85b; 86tl and b; 89br; 91br; 92t and c; 93br.

The publishers would like to thank the following individuals and picture agencies for kindly allowing their photographs to be reproduced for the purposes of this book:

Ed Gabriel: 10 (all).

Sara Rittershausen: 14; 15 (all); 16 (all); 17 (all); 19 (all).

Tim Shepherd: 12bl and br; 13 (all); 18br.

The vast majority of the orchids in this book were photographed at Burnham Nurseries Ltd., Forches Cross, Newton Abbot, TQ12 6PZ, in England, or on location in Thailand and Brazil.